The Iraq Study Group Report

The Iraq Study Group Report

James A. Baker, III, and
Lee H. Hamilton, Co-Chairs

Lawrence S. Eagleburger,
Vernon E. Jordan, Jr., Edwin Meese III,
Sandra Day O'Connor, Leon E. Panetta,
William J. Perry, Charles S. Robb,
Alan K. Simpson

VINTAGE BOOKS
A Division of Random House, Inc.
New York

FIRST VINTAGE BOOKS EDITION: DECEMBER 2006

The Authorized Edition of *The Iraq Study Group Report* is published in the United States by Vintage Books, a division of Random House, Inc., New York, and in Canada by Random House of Canada Limited, Toronto.

Maps © 2006 by Joyce Pendola

Vintage and colophon are registered trademarks of Random House, Inc.

ISBN: 0-307-38656-2

ISBN-13: 978-0-307-38656-4

www.vintagebooks.com

A portion of the proceeds from the purchase of this book will be donated to the National Military Family Association, the only nonprofit organization that represents the families of the Army, Navy, Air Force, Marine Corps, Coast Guard, and the Commissioned Corps of the Public Health Service and the National Oceanic and Atmospheric Administration, prepares spouses, children, and parents to better deal with the unique challenges of military life. The Association protects benefits vital to all families, including those of the deployed, wounded, and fallen. For more than 35 years, its staff and volunteers, comprised mostly of military family members, have built a reputation as the leading experts on military family issues. For more information, visit www.nmfa.org.

Printed in the United States of America
10 9 8 7 6 5 4 3 2 1

First Edition

Contents

Contents

II. The Way Forward—A New Approach

Contents

Appendices

Letter from the Co-Chairs

There is no magic formula to solve the problems of Iraq. However, there are actions that can be taken to improve the situation and protect American interests.

Many Americans are dissatisfied, not just with the situation in Iraq but with the state of our political debate regarding Iraq. Our political leaders must build a bipartisan approach to bring a responsible conclusion to what is now a lengthy and costly war. Our country deserves a debate that prizes substance over rhetoric, and a policy that is adequately funded and sustainable. The President and Congress must work together. Our leaders must be candid and forthright with the American people in order to win their support.

No one can guarantee that any course of action in Iraq at this point will stop sectarian warfare, growing violence, or a slide toward chaos. If current trends continue, the potential consequences are severe. Because of the role and responsibility of the United States in Iraq, and the commitments our government has made, the United States has special obligations. Our country must address as best it can Iraq's many problems.

The United States has long-term relationships and interests at stake in the Middle East, and needs to stay engaged.

In this consensus report, the ten members of the Iraq Study Group present a new approach because we believe there is a better way forward. All options have not been exhausted. We believe it is still possible to pursue different policies that can give Iraq an opportunity for a better future, combat terrorism, stabilize a critical region of the world, and protect America's credibility, interests, and values. Our report makes it clear that the Iraqi government and the Iraqi people also must act to achieve a stable and hopeful future.

What we recommend in this report demands a tremendous amount of political will and cooperation by the executive and legislative branches of the U.S. government. It demands skillful implementation. It demands unity of effort by government agencies. And its success depends on the unity of the American people in a time of political polarization. Americans can and must enjoy the right of robust debate within a democracy. Yet U.S. foreign policy is doomed to failure—as is any course of action in Iraq—if it is not supported by a broad, sustained consensus. The aim of our report is to move our country toward such a consensus.

We want to thank all those we have interviewed and those who have contributed information and assisted the Study Group, both inside and outside the U.S. government, in Iraq, and around the world. We thank the members of the expert working groups, and staff from the sponsoring organizations. We especially thank our colleagues on the Study Group, who have worked with us on these difficult issues in a spirit of generosity and bipartisanship.

Letter from the Co-Chairs

In presenting our report to the President, Congress, and the American people, we dedicate it to the men and women—military and civilian—who have served and are serving in Iraq, and to their families back home. They have demonstrated extraordinary courage and made difficult sacrifices. Every American is indebted to them.

We also honor the many Iraqis who have sacrificed on behalf of their country, and the members of the Coalition Forces who have stood with us and with the people of Iraq.

James A. Baker, III   Lee H. Hamilton

Executive Summary

The situation in Iraq is grave and deteriorating. There is no path that can guarantee success, but the prospects can be improved.

In this report, we make a number of recommendations for actions to be taken in Iraq, the United States, and the region. Our most important recommendations call for new and enhanced diplomatic and political efforts in Iraq and the region, and a change in the primary mission of U.S. forces in Iraq that will enable the United States to begin to move its combat forces out of Iraq responsibly. We believe that these two recommendations are equally important and reinforce one another. If they are effectively implemented, and if the Iraqi government moves forward with national reconciliation, Iraqis will have an opportunity for a better future, terrorism will be dealt a blow, stability will be enhanced in an important part of the world, and America's credibility, interests, and values will be protected.

The challenges in Iraq are complex. Violence is increasing in scope and lethality. It is fed by a Sunni Arab insurgency, Shiite militias and death squads, al Qaeda, and widespread criminality. Sectarian conflict is the principal challenge to stability.

The Iraqi people have a democratically elected government, yet it is not adequately advancing national reconciliation, providing basic security, or delivering essential services. Pessimism is pervasive.

If the situation continues to deteriorate, the consequences could be severe. A slide toward chaos could trigger the collapse of Iraq's government and a humanitarian catastrophe. Neighboring countries could intervene. Sunni-Shia clashes could spread. Al Qaeda could win a propaganda victory and expand its base of operations. The global standing of the United States could be diminished. Americans could become more polarized.

During the past nine months we have considered a full range of approaches for moving forward. All have flaws. Our recommended course has shortcomings, but we firmly believe that it includes the best strategies and tactics to positively influence the outcome in Iraq and the region.

External Approach

The policies and actions of Iraq's neighbors greatly affect its stability and prosperity. No country in the region will benefit in the long term from a chaotic Iraq. Yet Iraq's neighbors are not doing enough to help Iraq achieve stability. Some are undercutting stability.

The United States should immediately launch a new diplomatic offensive to build an international consensus for stability in Iraq and the region. This diplomatic effort should include every country that has an interest in avoiding a chaotic Iraq, including all of Iraq's neighbors. Iraq's neighbors and key states in and outside the region should form a support group to reinforce security and national reconciliation within Iraq, neither of which Iraq can achieve on its own.

Executive Summary

Given the ability of Iran and Syria to influence events within Iraq and their interest in avoiding chaos in Iraq, the United States should try to engage them constructively. In seeking to influence the behavior of both countries, the United States has disincentives and incentives available. Iran should stem the flow of arms and training to Iraq, respect Iraq's sovereignty and territorial integrity, and use its influence over Iraqi Shia groups to encourage national reconciliation. The issue of Iran's nuclear programs should continue to be dealt with by the five permanent members of the United Nations Security Council plus Germany. Syria should control its border with Iraq to stem the flow of funding, insurgents, and terrorists in and out of Iraq.

The United States cannot achieve its goals in the Middle East unless it deals directly with the Arab-Israeli conflict and regional instability. There must be a renewed and sustained commitment by the United States to a comprehensive Arab-Israeli peace on all fronts: Lebanon, Syria, and President Bush's June 2002 commitment to a two-state solution for Israel and Palestine. This commitment must include direct talks with, by, and between Israel, Lebanon, Palestinians (those who accept Israel's right to exist), and Syria.

As the United States develops its approach toward Iraq and the Middle East, the United States should provide additional political, economic, and military support for Afghanistan, including resources that might become available as combat forces are moved out of Iraq.

Internal Approach

The most important questions about Iraq's future are now the responsibility of Iraqis. The United States must adjust its role in Iraq to encourage the Iraqi people to take control of their own destiny.

The Iraqi government should accelerate assuming responsibility for Iraqi security by increasing the number and quality of Iraqi Army brigades. While this process is under way, and to facilitate it, the United States should significantly increase the number of U.S. military personnel, including combat troops, imbedded in and supporting Iraqi Army units. As these actions proceed, U.S. combat forces could begin to move out of Iraq.

The primary mission of U.S. forces in Iraq should evolve to one of supporting the Iraqi army, which would take over primary responsibility for combat operations. By the first quarter of 2008, subject to unexpected developments in the security situation on the ground, all combat brigades not necessary for force protection could be out of Iraq. At that time, U.S. combat forces in Iraq could be deployed only in units embedded with Iraqi forces, in rapid-reaction and special operations teams, and in training, equipping, advising, force protection, and search and rescue. Intelligence and support efforts would continue. A vital mission of those rapid reaction and special operations forces would be to undertake strikes against al Qaeda in Iraq.

It is clear that the Iraqi government will need assistance from the United States for some time to come, especially in carrying out security responsibilities. Yet the United States must make it clear to the Iraqi government that the United States could carry out its plans, including planned redeployments, even if the Iraqi government did not implement their planned changes. The United States must not make an open-ended commitment to keep large numbers of American troops deployed in Iraq.

Executive Summary

As redeployment proceeds, military leaders should emphasize training and education of forces that have returned to the United States in order to restore the force to full combat capability. As equipment returns to the United States, Congress should appropriate sufficient funds to restore the equipment over the next five years.

The United States should work closely with Iraq's leaders to support the achievement of specific objectives—or milestones—on national reconciliation, security, and governance. Miracles cannot be expected, but the people of Iraq have the right to expect action and progress. The Iraqi government needs to show its own citizens—and the citizens of the United States and other countries—that it deserves continued support.

Prime Minister Nouri al-Maliki, in consultation with the United States, has put forward a set of milestones critical for Iraq. His list is a good start, but it must be expanded to include milestones that can strengthen the government and benefit the Iraqi people. President Bush and his national security team should remain in close and frequent contact with the Iraqi leadership to convey a clear message: there must be prompt action by the Iraqi government to make substantial progress toward the achievement of these milestones.

If the Iraqi government demonstrates political will and makes substantial progress toward the achievement of milestones on national reconciliation, security, and governance, the United States should make clear its willingness to continue training, assistance, and support for Iraq's security forces and to continue political, military, and economic support. If the Iraqi government does not make substantial progress toward the achievement of milestones on national reconciliation, security, and governance, the United States should reduce its political, military, or economic support for the Iraqi government.

Our report makes recommendations in several other areas. They include improvements to the Iraqi criminal justice system, the Iraqi oil sector, the U.S. reconstruction efforts in Iraq, the U.S. budget process, the training of U.S. government personnel, and U.S. intelligence capabilities.

Conclusion

It is the unanimous view of the Iraq Study Group that these recommendations offer a new way forward for the United States in Iraq and the region. They are comprehensive and need to be implemented in a coordinated fashion. They should not be separated or carried out in isolation. The dynamics of the region are as important to Iraq as events within Iraq.

The challenges are daunting. There will be difficult days ahead. But by pursuing this new way forward, Iraq, the region, and the United States of America can emerge stronger.

I

Assessment

There is no guarantee for success in Iraq. The situation in Baghdad and several provinces is dire. Saddam Hussein has been removed from power and the Iraqi people have a democratically elected government that is broadly representative of Iraq's population, yet the government is not adequately advancing national reconciliation, providing basic security, or delivering essential services. The level of violence is high and growing. There is great suffering, and the daily lives of many Iraqis show little or no improvement. Pessimism is pervasive.

U.S. military and civilian personnel, and our coalition partners, are making exceptional and dedicated efforts—and sacrifices—to help Iraq. Many Iraqis have also made extraordinary efforts and sacrifices for a better future. However, the ability of the United States to influence events within Iraq is diminishing. Many Iraqis are embracing sectarian identities. The lack of security impedes economic development. Most countries in the region are not playing a constructive role in support of Iraq, and some are undercutting stability.

Iraq is vital to regional and even global stability, and is critical to U.S. interests. It runs along the sectarian fault lines of

Shia and Sunni Islam, and of Kurdish and Arab populations. It has the world's second-largest known oil reserves. It is now a base of operations for international terrorism, including al Qaeda.

Iraq is a centerpiece of American foreign policy, influencing how the United States is viewed in the region and around the world. Because of the gravity of Iraq's condition and the country's vital importance, the United States is facing one of its most difficult and significant international challenges in decades. Because events in Iraq have been set in motion by American decisions and actions, the United States has both a national and a moral interest in doing what it can to give Iraqis an opportunity to avert anarchy.

An assessment of the security, political, economic, and regional situation follows (all figures current as of publication), along with an assessment of the consequences if Iraq continues to deteriorate, and an analysis of some possible courses of action.

A. Assessment of the Current Situation in Iraq

1. Security

Attacks against U.S., Coalition, and Iraqi security forces are persistent and growing. October 2006 was the deadliest month for U.S. forces since January 2005, with 102 Americans killed. Total attacks in October 2006 averaged 180 per day, up from 70 per day in January 2006. Daily attacks against Iraqi security forces in October were more than double the level in January. Attacks against civilians in October were four times higher than in January. Some 3,000 Iraqi civilians are killed every month.

Sources of Violence

Violence is increasing in scope, complexity, and lethality. There are multiple sources of violence in Iraq: the Sunni Arab insurgency, al Qaeda and affiliated jihadist groups, Shiite militias and death squads, and organized criminality. Sectarian violence—particularly in and around Baghdad—has become the principal challenge to stability.

Most attacks on Americans still come from the Sunni Arab insurgency. The insurgency comprises former elements of the Saddam Hussein regime, disaffected Sunni Arab Iraqis, and common criminals. It has significant support within the Sunni Arab community. The insurgency has no single leadership but is a network of networks. It benefits from participants' detailed knowledge of Iraq's infrastructure, and arms and financing are supplied primarily from within Iraq. The insurgents have different goals, although nearly all oppose the presence of U.S. forces in Iraq. Most wish to restore Sunni Arab rule in the country. Some aim at winning local power and control.

Al Qaeda is responsible for a small portion of the violence in Iraq, but that includes some of the more spectacular acts: suicide attacks, large truck bombs, and attacks on significant religious or political targets. Al Qaeda in Iraq is now largely Iraqi-run and composed of Sunni Arabs. Foreign fighters—numbering an estimated 1,300—play a supporting role or carry out suicide operations. Al Qaeda's goals include instigating a wider sectarian war between Iraq's Sunni and Shia, and driving the United States out of Iraq.

Sectarian violence causes the largest number of Iraqi civilian casualties. Iraq is in the grip of a deadly cycle: Sunni insurgent attacks spark large-scale Shia reprisals, and vice versa. Groups of Iraqis are often found bound and executed, their bodies dumped in rivers or fields. The perception of unchecked violence emboldens militias, shakes confidence in the government, and leads Iraqis to flee to places where their sect is the majority and where they feel they are in less danger. In some parts of Iraq—notably in Baghdad—sectarian cleansing is taking place. The United Nations estimates that 1.6 million are displaced within Iraq, and up to 1.8 million Iraqis have fled the country.

Shiite militias engaging in sectarian violence pose a substantial threat to immediate and long-term stability. These militias are diverse. Some are affiliated with the government, some are highly localized, and some are wholly outside the law. They are fragmenting, with an increasing breakdown in command structure. The militias target Sunni Arab civilians, and some struggle for power in clashes with one another. Some even target government ministries. They undermine the authority of the Iraqi government and security forces, as well as the ability of Sunnis to join a peaceful political process. The prevalence of militias sends a powerful message: political leaders can preserve and expand their power only if backed by armed force.

The Mahdi Army, led by Moqtada al-Sadr, may number as many as 60,000 fighters. It has directly challenged U.S. and Iraqi government forces, and it is widely believed to engage in regular violence against Sunni Arab civilians. Mahdi fighters patrol certain Shia enclaves, notably northeast Baghdad's teeming neighborhood of 2.5 million known as "Sadr City." As the Mahdi Army has grown in size and influence, some elements have moved beyond Sadr's control.

The Badr Brigade is affiliated with the Supreme Council for the Islamic Revolution in Iraq (SCIRI), which is led by Abdul Aziz al-Hakim. The Badr Brigade has long-standing ties with the Iranian Revolutionary Guard Corps. Many Badr members have become integrated into the Iraqi police, and others play policing roles in southern Iraqi cities. While wearing the uniform of the security services, Badr fighters have targeted Sunni Arab civilians. Badr fighters have also clashed with the Mahdi Army, particularly in southern Iraq.

Criminality also makes daily life unbearable for many Iraqis. Robberies, kidnappings, and murder are commonplace in much of the country. Organized criminal rackets thrive, particularly in unstable areas like Anbar province. Some criminal gangs cooperate with, finance, or purport to be part of the

Sunni insurgency or a Shiite militia in order to gain legitimacy. As one knowledgeable American official put it, "If there were foreign forces in New Jersey, Tony Soprano would be an insurgent leader."

Four of Iraq's eighteen provinces are highly insecure— Baghdad, Anbar, Diyala, and Salah ad Din. These provinces account for about 40 percent of Iraq's population of 26 million. In Baghdad, the violence is largely between Sunni and Shia. In Anbar, the violence is attributable to the Sunni insurgency and to al Qaeda, and the situation is deteriorating.

In Kirkuk, the struggle is between Kurds, Arabs, and Turkmen. In Basra and the south, the violence is largely an intra-Shia power struggle. The most stable parts of the country are the three provinces of the Kurdish north and parts of the Shia south. However, most of Iraq's cities have a sectarian mix and are plagued by persistent violence.

U.S., Coalition, and Iraqi Forces

Confronting this violence are the Multi-National Forces–Iraq under U.S. command, working in concert with Iraq's security forces. The Multi-National Forces–Iraq were authorized by UN Security Council Resolution 1546 in 2004, and the mandate was extended in November 2006 for another year.

Approximately 141,000 U.S. military personnel are serving in Iraq, together with approximately 16,500 military personnel from twenty-seven coalition partners, the largest contingent being 7,200 from the United Kingdom. The U.S. Army has principal responsibility for Baghdad and the north. The U.S. Marine Corps takes the lead in Anbar province. The United Kingdom has responsibility in the southeast, chiefly in Basra.

Along with this military presence, the United States is

building its largest embassy in Baghdad. The current U.S. embassy in Baghdad totals about 1,000 U.S. government employees. There are roughly 5,000 civilian contractors in the country.

Currently, the U.S. military rarely engages in large-scale combat operations. Instead, counterinsurgency efforts focus on a strategy of "clear, hold, and build"—"clearing" areas of insurgents and death squads, "holding" those areas with Iraqi security forces, and "building" areas with quick-impact reconstruction projects.

Nearly every U.S. Army and Marine combat unit, and several National Guard and Reserve units, have been to Iraq at least once. Many are on their second or even third rotations; rotations are typically one year for Army units, seven months for Marine units. Regular rotations, in and out of Iraq or within the country, complicate brigade and battalion efforts to get to know the local scene, earn the trust of the population, and build a sense of cooperation.

Many military units are under significant strain. Because the harsh conditions in Iraq are wearing out equipment more quickly than anticipated, many units do not have fully functional equipment for training when they redeploy to the United States. An extraordinary amount of sacrifice has been asked of our men and women in uniform, and of their families. The American military has little reserve force to call on if it needs ground forces to respond to other crises around the world.

A primary mission of U.S. military strategy in Iraq is the training of competent Iraqi security forces. By the end of 2006, the Multi-National Security Transition Command–Iraq under American leadership is expected to have trained and equipped a target number of approximately 326,000 Iraqi security services. That figure includes 138,000 members of the Iraqi Army and 188,000 Iraqi police. Iraqis have operational control over roughly one-third of Iraqi security forces; the U.S. has operational control over most of the rest. No U.S. forces are under Iraqi command.

The Iraqi Army

The Iraqi Army is making fitful progress toward becoming a reliable and disciplined fighting force loyal to the national government. By the end of 2006, the Iraqi Army is expected to comprise 118 battalions formed into 36 brigades under the command of 10 divisions. Although the Army is one of the more professional Iraqi institutions, its performance has been uneven. The training numbers are impressive, but they represent only part of the story.

Significant questions remain about the ethnic composition and loyalties of some Iraqi units—specifically, whether they will carry out missions on behalf of national goals instead of a sectarian agenda. Of Iraq's 10 planned divisions, those that are even-numbered are made up of Iraqis who signed up to serve in a specific area, and they have been reluctant to redeploy to other areas of the country. As a result, elements of the Army have refused to carry out missions.

The Iraqi Army is also confronted by several other significant challenges:

- Units lack leadership. They lack the ability to work together and perform at higher levels of organization—the brigade and division level. Leadership training and the experience of leadership are the essential elements to improve performance.

- Units lack equipment. They cannot carry out their missions without adequate equipment. Congress has been generous in funding requests for U.S. troops, but it has resisted fully funding Iraqi forces. The entire appropriation for Iraqi defense forces for FY 2006 ($3 billion) is less than the United States currently spends in Iraq every two weeks.

- Units lack personnel. Soldiers are on leave one week a month so that they can visit their families and take them their pay. Soldiers are paid in cash because there is no banking system. Soldiers are given leave liberally and face no penalties for absence without leave. Unit readiness rates are low, often at 50 percent or less.

- Units lack logistics and support. They lack the ability to sustain their operations, the capability to transport supplies and troops, and the capacity to provide their own indirect fire support, close-air support, technical intelligence, and medical evacuation. They will depend on the United States for logistics and support through at least 2007.

The Iraqi Police

The state of the Iraqi police is substantially worse than that of the Iraqi Army. The Iraqi Police Service currently numbers roughly 135,000 and is responsible for local policing. It has neither the training nor legal authority to conduct criminal investigations, nor the firepower to take on organized crime, insurgents, or militias. The Iraqi National Police numbers roughly 25,000 and its officers have been trained in counterinsurgency operations, not police work. The Border Enforcement Department numbers roughly 28,000.

Iraqi police cannot control crime, and they routinely engage in sectarian violence, including the unnecessary detention, torture, and targeted execution of Sunni Arab civilians. The police are organized under the Ministry of the Interior, which is confronted by corruption and militia infiltration and lacks control over police in the provinces.

The United States and the Iraqi government recognize the importance of reform. The current Minister of the Interior has called for purging militia members and criminals from the police. But he has little police experience or base of support. There is no clear Iraqi or U.S. agreement on the character and mission of the police. U.S. authorities do not know with precision the composition and membership of the various police forces, nor the disposition of their funds and equipment. There are ample reports of Iraqi police officers participating in training in order to obtain a weapon, uniform, and ammunition for use in sectarian violence. Some are on the payroll but don't show up for work. In the words of a senior American general, "2006 was supposed to be 'the year of the police' but it hasn't materialized that way."

Facilities Protection Services

The Facilities Protection Service poses additional problems. Each Iraqi ministry has an armed unit, ostensibly to guard the ministry's infrastructure. All together, these units total roughly 145,000 uniformed Iraqis under arms. However, these units have questionable loyalties and capabilities. In the ministries of Health, Agriculture, and Transportation—controlled by Moqtada al-Sadr—the Facilities Protection Service is a source of funding and jobs for the Mahdi Army. One senior U.S. official described the Facilities Protection Service as "incompetent, dysfunctional, or subversive." Several Iraqis simply referred to them as militias.

The Iraqi government has begun to bring the Facilities Protection Service under the control of the Interior Ministry. The intention is to identify and register Facilities Protection personnel, standardize their treatment, and provide some training. Though the approach is reasonable, this effort may exceed the current capability of the Interior Ministry.

Operation Together Forward II

In a major effort to quell the violence in Iraq, U.S. military forces joined with Iraqi forces to establish security in Baghdad with an operation called "Operation Together Forward II," which began in August 2006. Under Operation Together Forward II, U.S. forces are working with members of the Iraqi Army and police to "clear, hold, and build" in Baghdad, moving neighborhood by neighborhood. There are roughly 15,000 U.S. troops in Baghdad.

This operation—and the security of Baghdad—is crucial to security in Iraq more generally. A capital city of more than 6 million, Baghdad contains some 25 percent of the country's population. It is the largest Sunni and Shia city in Iraq. It has high concentrations of both Sunni insurgents and Shiite militias. Both Iraqi and American leaders told us that as Baghdad goes, so goes Iraq.

The results of Operation Together Forward II are disheartening. Violence in Baghdad—already at high levels—jumped more than 43 percent between the summer and October 2006. U.S. forces continue to suffer high casualties. Perpetrators of violence leave neighborhoods in advance of security sweeps, only to filter back later. Iraqi police have been unable or unwilling to stop such infiltration and continuing violence. The Iraqi Army has provided only two out of the six battalions that it promised in August would join American forces in Baghdad. The Iraqi government has rejected sustained security operations in Sadr City.

Security efforts will fail unless the Iraqis have both the capability to hold areas that have been cleared and the will to clear neighborhoods that are home to Shiite militias. U.S. forces can "clear" any neighborhood, but there are neither enough U.S. troops present nor enough support from Iraqi security forces to "hold" neighborhoods so cleared. The same holds true for the rest of Iraq. Because none of the operations conducted by U.S. and Iraqi military forces are fundamentally changing the conditions encouraging the sectarian violence, U.S. forces seem to be caught in a mission that has no foreseeable end.

2. Politics

Iraq is a sovereign state with a democratically elected Council of Representatives. A government of national unity was formed in May 2006 that is broadly representative of the Iraqi people. Iraq has ratified a constitution, and—per agreement with Sunni Arab leaders—has initiated a process of review to determine if the constitution needs amendment.

The composition of the Iraqi government is basically sectarian, and key players within the government too often act in their sectarian interest. Iraq's Shia, Sunni, and Kurdish leaders frequently fail to demonstrate the political will to act in Iraq's national interest, and too many Iraqi ministries lack the capacity to govern effectively. The result is an even weaker central government than the constitution provides.

There is widespread Iraqi, American, and international agreement on the key issues confronting the Iraqi government: national reconciliation, including the negotiation of a "political deal" among Iraq's sectarian groups on Constitution review, de-Baathification, oil revenue sharing, provincial elections, the future of Kirkuk, and amnesty; security, particularly curbing militias and reducing the violence in Baghdad; and governance, including the provision of basic services and the rollback of pervasive corruption. Because Iraqi leaders view issues through a sectarian prism, we will summarize the differing perspectives of Iraq's main sectarian groups.

Sectarian Viewpoints

The Shia, the majority of Iraq's population, have gained power for the first time in more than 1,300 years. Above all, many Shia are interested in preserving that power. However, fissures have emerged within the broad Shia coalition, known as the United Iraqi Alliance. Shia factions are struggling for power—over regions, ministries, and Iraq as a whole. The difficulties in holding together a broad and fractious coalition have led several observers in Baghdad to comment that Shia leaders are held "hostage to extremes." Within the coalition as a whole, there is a reluctance to reach a political accommodation with the Sunnis or to disarm Shiite militias.

Prime Minister Nouri al-Maliki has demonstrated an understanding of the key issues facing Iraq, notably the need for national reconciliation and security in Baghdad. Yet strains have emerged between Maliki's government and the United

States. Maliki has publicly rejected a U.S. timetable to achieve certain benchmarks, ordered the removal of blockades around Sadr City, sought more control over Iraqi security forces, and resisted U.S. requests to move forward on reconciliation or on disbanding Shiite militias.

Sistani, Sadr, Hakim

The U.S. deals primarily with the Iraqi government, but the most powerful Shia figures in Iraq do not hold national office. Of the following three vital power brokers in the Shia community, the United States is unable to talk directly with one (Grand Ayatollah Ali al-Sistani) and does not talk to another (Moqtada al-Sadr).

GRAND AYATOLLAH ALI AL-SISTANI: Sistani is the leading Shiite cleric in Iraq. Despite staying out of day-to-day politics, he has been the most influential leader in the country: all major Shia leaders have sought his approval or guidance. Sistani has encouraged a unified Shia bloc with moderated aims within a unified Iraq. Sistani's influence may be waning, as his words have not succeeded in preventing intra-Shia violence or retaliation against Sunnis.

ABDUL AZIZ AL-HAKIM: Hakim is a cleric and the leader of the Supreme Council for the Islamic Revolution in Iraq (SCIRI), the largest and most organized Shia political party. It seeks the creation of an autonomous Shia region comprising nine provinces in the south. Hakim has consistently protected and advanced his party's position. SCIRI has close ties with Iran.

MOQTADA AL-SADR: Sadr has a large following among impoverished Shia, particularly in Baghdad. He has joined Maliki's governing coalition, but his Mahdi Army has clashed with the Badr Brigades, as well as with Iraqi, U.S., and U.K. forces. Sadr claims to be an Iraqi nationalist. Several observers remarked to us that Sadr was following the model of Hezbollah in Lebanon: building a political party that controls basic services within the government and an armed militia outside of the government.

Sunni Arabs feel displaced because of the loss of their traditional position of power in Iraq. They are torn, unsure whether to seek their aims through political participation or through violent insurgency. They remain angry about U.S. decisions to dissolve Iraqi security forces and to pursue the "de-Baathification" of Iraq's government and society. Sunnis are confronted by paradoxes: they have opposed the presence of U.S. forces in Iraq but need those forces to protect them against Shia militias; they chafe at being governed by a majority Shia administration but reject a federal, decentralized Iraq and do not see a Sunni autonomous region as feasible for themselves.

Hashimi and Dhari

The influence of Sunni Arab politicians in the government is questionable. The leadership of the Sunni Arab insurgency is murky, but the following two key Sunni Arab figures have broad support.

TARIQ AL-HASHIMI: Hashimi is one of two vice presidents of Iraq and the head of the Iraqi Islamic Party, the largest Sunni Muslim bloc in parliament. Hashimi opposes the formation of autonomous regions and has advocated the distribution of oil revenues based on population, a reversal of de-Baathification, and the removal of Shiite militia fighters from the Iraqi security forces. Shiite death squads have recently killed three of his siblings.

SHEIK HARITH AL-DHARI: Dhari is the head of the Muslim Scholars Association, the most influential Sunni organization in Iraq. Dhari has condemned the American occupation and spoken out against the Iraqi government. His organization has ties both to the Sunni Arab insurgency and to Sunnis within the Iraqi government. A warrant was recently issued for his arrest for inciting violence and terrorism, an act that sparked bitter Sunni protests across Iraq.

Iraqi Kurds have succeeded in presenting a united front of two main political blocs—the Kurdistan Democratic Party (KDP) and the Patriotic Union of Kurdistan (PUK). The Kurds have secured a largely autonomous Kurdish region in the north, and have achieved a prominent role for Kurds within the national government. Barzani leads the Kurdish regional government, and Talabani is president of Iraq.

Leading Kurdish politicians told us they preferred to be within a democratic, federal Iraqi state because an independent Kurdistan would be surrounded by hostile neighbors. However, a majority of Kurds favor independence. The Kurds have their own security forces—the *peshmerga*—which number roughly 100,000. They believe they could accommodate themselves to either a unified or a fractured Iraq.

Barzani and Talabani

Kurdish politics has been dominated for years by two figures who have long-standing ties in movements for Kurdish independence and self-government.

MASSOUD BARZANI: Barzani is the leader of the Kurdistan Democratic Party and the President of the Kurdish regional government. Barzani has cooperated with his longtime rival, Jalal Talabani, in securing an empowered, autonomous Kurdish region in northern Iraq. Barzani has ordered the lowering of Iraqi flags and raising of Kurdish flags in Kurdish-controlled areas.

JALAL TALABANI: Talabani is the leader of the Patriotic Union of Kurdistan and the President of Iraq. Whereas Barzani has focused his efforts in Kurdistan, Talabani has secured power in Baghdad, and several important PUK government ministers are loyal to him. Talabani strongly supports autonomy for Kurdistan. He has also sought to bring real power to the office of the presidency.

Key Issues

NATIONAL RECONCILIATION.   Prime Minister Maliki outlined a commendable program of national reconciliation soon after he entered office. However, the Iraqi government has not taken action on the key elements of national reconciliation: revising de-Baathification, which prevents many Sunni Arabs from participating in governance and society; providing amnesty for those who have fought against the government; sharing the country's oil revenues; demobilizing militias; amending the constitution; and settling the future of Kirkuk.

One core issue is federalism. The Iraqi Constitution, which created a largely autonomous Kurdistan region, allows other such regions to be established later, perhaps including a "Shi'astan" comprising nine southern provinces. This highly decentralized structure is favored by the Kurds and many Shia (particularly supporters of Abdul Aziz al-Hakim), but it is anathema to Sunnis. First, Sunni Arabs are generally Iraqi nationalists, albeit within the context of an Iraq they believe they should govern. Second, because Iraq's energy resources are in the Kurdish and Shia regions, there is no economically feasible "Sunni region." Particularly contentious is a provision in the constitution that shares revenues nationally from current oil reserves, while allowing revenues from reserves discovered in the future to go to the regions.

The Sunnis did not actively participate in the constitution-drafting process, and acceded to entering the government only on the condition that the constitution be amended. In September, the parliament agreed to initiate a constitutional review commission slated to complete its work within one year; it delayed considering the question of forming a federalized region in southern Iraq for eighteen months.

Another key unresolved issue is the future of Kirkuk, an oil-rich city in northern Iraq that is home to substantial numbers of Kurds, Arabs, and Turkmen. The Kurds insisted that the constitution require a popular referendum by December 2007 to determine whether Kirkuk can formally join the Kurdish administered region, an outcome that Arabs and Turkmen in Kirkuk staunchly oppose. The risks of further violence sparked by a Kirkuk referendum are great.

Iraq's leaders often claim that they do not want a division of the country, but we found that key Shia and Kurdish leaders have little commitment to national reconciliation. One prominent Shia leader told us pointedly that the current government has the support of 80 percent of the population, notably excluding Sunni Arabs. Kurds have fought for independence for decades, and when our Study Group visited Iraq, the leader of the Kurdish region ordered the lowering of Iraqi flags and the raising of Kurdish flags. One senior American general commented that the Iraqis "still do not know what kind of country they want to have." Yet many of Iraq's most powerful and well-positioned leaders are not working toward a united Iraq.

SECURITY. The security situation cannot improve unless leaders act in support of national reconciliation. Shiite leaders must make the decision to demobilize militias. Sunni Arabs must make the decision to seek their aims through a peaceful political process, not through violent revolt. The Iraqi government and Sunni Arab tribes must aggressively pursue al Qaeda.

Militias are currently seen as legitimate vehicles of political action. Shia political leaders make distinctions between the Sunni insurgency (which seeks to overthrow the government) and Shia militias (which are used to fight Sunnis, secure neighborhoods, and maximize power within the government). Though Prime Minister Maliki has said he will address the problem of militias, he has taken little meaningful action to curb their influence. He owes his office in large part to Sadr and has shown little willingness to take on him or his Mahdi Army.

Sunni Arabs have not made the strategic decision to abandon violent insurgency in favor of the political process. Sunni politicians within the government have a limited level of support and influence among their own population, and questionable influence over the insurgency. Insurgents wage a campaign of intimidation against Sunni leaders—assassinating the family members of those who do participate in the government. Too often, insurgents tolerate and cooperate with al Qaeda, as they share a mutual interest in attacking U.S. and Shia forces. However, Sunni Arab tribal leaders in Anbar province recently took the positive step of agreeing to pursue al Qaeda and foreign fighters in their midst, and have started to take action on those commitments.

Sunni politicians told us that the U.S. military has to take on the militias; Shia politicians told us that the U.S. military has to help them take out the Sunni insurgents and al Qaeda. Each side watches the other. Sunni insurgents will not lay down arms unless the Shia militias are disarmed. Shia militias will not disarm until the Sunni insurgency is destroyed. To put it simply: there are many armed groups within Iraq, and very little will to lay down arms.

GOVERNANCE.   The Iraqi government is not effectively providing its people with basic services: electricity, drinking water, sewage, health care, and education. In many sectors, production is below or hovers around prewar levels. In Baghdad and other unstable areas, the situation is much worse. There are five major reasons for this problem.

First, the government sometimes provides services on a sectarian basis. For example, in one Sunni neighborhood of Shia-governed Baghdad, there is less than two hours of electricity each day and trash piles are waist-high. One American official told us that Baghdad is run like a "Shia dictatorship" because Sunnis boycotted provincial elections in 2005, and therefore are not represented in local government.

Second, security is lacking. Insurgents target key infrastructure. For instance, electricity transmission towers are downed by explosives, and then sniper attacks prevent repairs from being made.

Third, corruption is rampant. One senior Iraqi official estimated that official corruption costs Iraq $5–7 billion per year. Notable steps have been taken: Iraq has a functioning audit board and inspectors general in the ministries, and senior leaders including the Prime Minister have identified rooting out corruption as a national priority. But too many political leaders still pursue their personal, sectarian, or party interests. There are still no examples of senior officials who have been brought before a court of law and convicted on corruption charges.

Fourth, capacity is inadequate. Most of Iraq's technocratic class was pushed out of the government as part of de-Baathification. Other skilled Iraqis have fled the country as violence has risen. Too often, Iraq's elected representatives treat the ministries as political spoils. Many ministries can do little more than pay salaries, spending as little as 10–15 percent of their capital budget. They lack technical expertise and suffer from corruption, inefficiency, a banking system that does not permit the transfer of moneys, extensive red tape put in place in part to deter corruption, and a Ministry of Finance reluctant to disburse funds.

Fifth, the judiciary is weak. Much has been done to establish an Iraqi judiciary, including a supreme court, and Iraq has some dedicated judges. But criminal investigations are conducted by magistrates, and they are too few and inadequately trained to perform this function. Intimidation of the Iraqi judiciary has been ruthless. As one senior U.S. official said to us, "We can protect judges, but not their families, their extended families, their friends." Many Iraqis feel that crime not only is unpunished, it is rewarded.

3. Economics

There has been some economic progress in Iraq, and Iraq has tremendous potential for growth. But economic development is hobbled by insecurity, corruption, lack of investment, dilapidated infrastructure, and uncertainty. As one U.S. official observed to us, Iraq's economy has been badly shocked and is dysfunctional after suffering decades of problems: Iraq had a police state economy in the 1970s, a war economy in the 1980s, and a sanctions economy in the 1990s. Immediate and long-term growth depends predominantly on the oil sector.

Economic Performance

There are some encouraging signs. Currency reserves are stable and growing at $12 billion. Consumer imports of computers, cell phones, and other appliances have increased dramatically. New businesses are opening, and construction is moving forward in secure areas. Because of Iraq's ample oil reserves, water resources, and fertile lands, significant growth is possible if violence is reduced and the capacity of government improves. For example, wheat yields increased more than 40 percent in Kurdistan during this past year.

The Iraqi government has also made progress in meeting benchmarks set by the International Monetary Fund. Most prominently, subsidies have been reduced—for instance, the price per liter of gas has increased from roughly 1.7 cents to 23 cents (a figure far closer to regional prices). However, energy and food subsidies generally remain a burden, costing Iraq $11 billion per year.

Despite the positive signs, many leading economic indicators are negative. Instead of meeting a target of 10 percent, growth in Iraq is at roughly 4 percent this year. Inflation is above 50 percent. Unemployment estimates range widely from 20 to 60 percent. The investment climate is bleak, with foreign direct investment under 1 percent of GDP. Too many Iraqis do not see tangible improvements in their daily economic situation.

Oil Sector

Oil production and sales account for nearly 70 percent of Iraq's GDP, and more than 95 percent of government revenues. Iraq produces around 2.2 million barrels per day, and exports about 1.5 million barrels per day. This is below both prewar production levels and the Iraqi government's target of 2.5 million barrels per day, and far short of the vast potential of the Iraqi oil sector. Fortunately for the government, global energy prices have been higher than projected, making it possible for Iraq to meet its budget revenue targets.

Problems with oil production are caused by lack of security, lack of investment, and lack of technical capacity. Insurgents with a detailed knowledge of Iraq's infrastructure target pipelines and oil facilities. There is no metering system for the oil. There is poor maintenance at pumping stations, pipelines, and port facilities, as well as inadequate investment in modern technology. Iraq had a cadre of experts in the oil sector, but intimidation and an extended migration of experts to other countries have eroded technical capacity. Foreign companies have been reluctant to invest, and Iraq's Ministry of Oil has been unable to spend more than 15 percent of its capital budget.

Corruption is also debilitating. Experts estimate that 150,000 to 200,000—and perhaps as many as 500,000—barrels of oil per day are being stolen. Controlled prices for refined products result in shortages within Iraq, which drive consumers to the thriving black market. One senior U.S. official told us that corruption is more responsible than insurgents for breakdowns in the oil sector.

The Politics of Oil

The politics of oil has the potential to further damage the country's already fragile efforts to create a unified central government. The Iraqi Constitution leaves the door open for regions to take the lead in developing new oil resources. Article 108 states that "oil and gas are the ownership of all the peoples of Iraq in all the regions and governorates," while Article 109 tasks the federal government with "the management of oil and gas extracted from current fields." This language has led to contention over what constitutes a "new" or an "existing" resource, a question that has profound ramifications for the ultimate control of future oil revenue.

Senior members of Iraq's oil industry argue that a national oil company could reduce political tensions by centralizing revenues and reducing regional or local claims to a percentage of the revenue derived from production. However, regional leaders are suspicious and resist this proposal, affirming the rights of local communities to have direct access to the inflow of oil revenue. Kurdish leaders have been particularly aggressive in asserting independent control of their oil assets, signing and implementing investment deals with foreign oil companies in northern Iraq. Shia politicians are also reported to be negotiating oil investment contracts with foreign companies.

There are proposals to redistribute a portion of oil revenues directly to the population on a per capita basis. These proposals have the potential to give all Iraqi citizens a stake in the nation's chief natural resource, but it would take time to develop a fair distribution system. Oil revenues have been incorporated into state budget projections for the next several years. There is no institution in Iraq at present that could properly implement such a distribution system. It would take substantial time to establish, and would have to be based on a well-developed state census and income tax system, which Iraq currently lacks.

U.S.-Led Reconstruction Efforts

The United States has appropriated a total of about $34 billion to support the reconstruction of Iraq, of which about $21 billion has been appropriated for the "Iraq Relief and Reconstruction Fund." Nearly $16 billion has been spent, and almost all the funds have been committed. The administration requested $1.6 billion for reconstruction in FY 2006, and received $1.485 billion. The administration requested $750 million for FY 2007. The trend line for economic assistance in FY 2008 also appears downward.

Congress has little appetite for appropriating more funds for reconstruction. There is a substantial need for continued reconstruction in Iraq, but serious questions remain about the capacity of the U.S. and Iraqi governments.

The coordination of assistance programs by the Defense Department, State Department, United States Agency for International Development, and other agencies has been ineffective. There are no clear lines establishing who is in charge of reconstruction.

As resources decline, the U.S. reconstruction effort is changing its focus, shifting from infrastructure, education, and health to smaller-scale ventures that are chosen and to some degree managed by local communities. A major attempt is also being made to improve the capacity of government bureaucracies at the national, regional, and provincial levels to provide services to the population as well as to select and manage infrastructure projects.

The United States has people embedded in several Iraqi ministries, but it confronts problems with access and sustainability. Moqtada al-Sadr objects to the U.S. presence in Iraq, and therefore the ministries he controls—Health, Agriculture, and Transportation—will not work with Americans. It is not clear that Iraqis can or will maintain and operate reconstruction projects launched by the United States.

Several senior military officers commented to us that the Commander's Emergency Response Program, which funds quick-impact projects such as the clearing of sewage and the restoration of basic services, is vital. The U.S. Agency for International Development, in contrast, is focused on long-term economic development and capacity building, but funds have not been committed to support these efforts into the future. The State Department leads seven Provincial Reconstruction Teams operating around the country. These teams can have a positive effect in secure areas, but not in areas where their work is hampered by significant security constraints.

Substantial reconstruction funds have also been provided to contractors, and the Special Inspector General for Iraq Reconstruction has documented numerous instances of waste and abuse. They have not all been put right. Contracting has gradually improved, as more oversight has been exercised and fewer cost-plus contracts have been granted; in addition, the use of Iraqi contractors has enabled the employment of more Iraqis in reconstruction projects.

4. International Support

International support for Iraqi reconstruction has been tepid. International donors pledged $13.5 billion to support reconstruction, but less than $4 billion has been delivered.

An important agreement with the Paris Club relieved a significant amount of Iraq's government debt and put the country on firmer financial footing. But the Gulf States, including Saudi Arabia and Kuwait, hold large amounts of Iraqi debt that they have not forgiven.

The United States is currently working with the United Nations and other partners to fashion the "International Compact" on Iraq. The goal is to provide Iraqis with greater debt relief and credits from the Gulf States, as well as to deliver on pledged aid from international donors. In return, the Iraqi government will agree to achieve certain economic reform milestones, such as building anticorruption measures into Iraqi institutions, adopting a fair legal framework for foreign investors, and reaching economic self-sufficiency by 2012. Several U.S. and international officials told us that the compact could be an opportunity to seek greater international engagement in the country.

The Region

The policies and actions of Iraq's neighbors greatly influence its stability and prosperity. No country in the region wants a chaotic Iraq. Yet Iraq's neighbors are doing little to help it, and some are undercutting its stability. Iraqis complain that neighbors are meddling in their affairs. When asked which of Iraq's neighbors are intervening in Iraq, one senior Iraqi official replied, "All of them."

The situation in Iraq is linked with events in the region. U.S. efforts in Afghanistan have been complicated by the overriding focus of U.S. attention and resources on Iraq. Several Iraqi, U.S., and international officials commented to us that Iraqi opposition to the United States—and support for Sadr—spiked in the aftermath of Israel's bombing campaign in Lebanon. The actions of Syria and Iran in Iraq are often tied to their broader concerns with the United States. Many Sunni Arab states are concerned about rising Iranian influence in Iraq and the region. Most of the region's countries are wary of U.S. efforts to promote democracy in Iraq and the Middle East.

Neighboring States

IRAN.   Of all the neighbors, Iran has the most leverage in Iraq. Iran has long-standing ties to many Iraqi Shia politicians, many of whom were exiled to Iran during the Saddam Hussein regime. Iran has provided arms, financial support, and training for Shiite militias within Iraq, as well as political support for Shia parties. There are also reports that Iran has supplied improvised explosive devices to groups—including Sunni Arab insurgents—that attack U.S. forces. The Iranian border with Iraq is porous, and millions of Iranians travel to Iraq each year to visit Shia holy sites. Many Iraqis spoke of Iranian meddling, and Sunnis took a particularly alarmist view. One leading Sunni politician told us, "If you turn over any stone in Iraq today, you will find Iran underneath."

U.S., Iraqi, and international officials also commented on the range of tensions between the United States and Iran, including Iran's nuclear program, Iran's support for terrorism, Iran's influence in Lebanon and the region, and Iran's influence in Iraq. Iran appears content for the U.S. military to be tied down in Iraq, a position that limits U.S. options in addressing Iran's nuclear program and allows Iran leverage over stability in Iraq. Proposed talks between Iran and the United States about the situation in Iraq have not taken place. One Iraqi official told us: "Iran is negotiating with the United States in the streets of Baghdad."

SYRIA.   Syria is also playing a counterproductive role. Iraqis are upset about what they perceive as Syrian support for efforts to undermine the Iraqi government. The Syrian role is not so much to take active measures as to countenance malign neglect: the Syrians look the other way as arms and foreign fighters flow across their border into Iraq, and former Baathist leaders find a safe haven within Syria. Like Iran, Syria is content to see the United States tied down in Iraq. That said, the Syrians have indicated that they want a dialogue with the United States, and in November 2006 agreed to restore diplomatic relations with Iraq after a 24-year break.

SAUDI ARABIA AND THE GULF STATES.   These countries for the most part have been passive and disengaged. They have declined to provide debt relief or substantial economic assistance to the Iraqi government. Several Iraqi Sunni Arab politicians complained that Saudi Arabia has not provided political support for their fellow Sunnis within Iraq. One observed that Saudi Arabia did not even send a letter when the Iraqi government was formed, whereas Iran has an ambassador in Iraq. Funding for the Sunni insurgency comes from private individuals within Saudi Arabia and the Gulf States, even as those governments help facilitate U.S. military operations in Iraq by providing basing and overflight rights and by cooperating on intelligence issues.

As worries about Iraq increase, the Gulf States are becoming more active. The United Arab Emirates and Kuwait have hosted meetings in support of the International Compact. Saudi Arabia recently took the positive step of hosting a conference of Iraqi religious leaders in Mecca. Several Gulf States have helped foster dialogue with Iraq's Sunni Arab population. While the Gulf States are not proponents of democracy in Iraq, they worry about the direction of events: battle-hardened insurgents from Iraq could pose a threat to their own internal stability, and the growth of Iranian influence in the region is deeply troubling to them.

TURKEY.   Turkish policy toward Iraq is focused on discouraging Kurdish nationalism, which is seen as an existential threat to Turkey's own internal stability. The Turks have supported the Turkmen minority within Iraq and have used their influence to try to block the incorporation of Kirkuk into Iraqi Kurdistan. At the same time, Turkish companies have invested in Kurdish areas in northern Iraq, and Turkish and Kurdish leaders have sought constructive engagement on political, security, and economic issues.

The Turks are deeply concerned about the operations of the Kurdish Workers Party (PKK)—a terrorist group based in northern Iraq that has killed thousands of Turks. They are upset that the United States and Iraq have not targeted the PKK more aggressively. The Turks have threatened to go after the PKK themselves, and have made several forays across the border into Iraq.

JORDAN AND EGYPT.   Both Jordan and Egypt have provided some assistance for the Iraqi government. Jordan has trained thousands of Iraqi police, has an ambassador in Baghdad, and King Abdullah recently hosted a meeting in Amman between President Bush and Prime Minister Maliki. Egypt has provided some limited Iraqi army training. Both Jordan and Egypt have facilitated U.S. military operations—Jordan by allowing overflight and search-and-rescue operations, Egypt by allowing overflight and Suez Canal transits; both provide important cooperation on intelligence. Jordan is currently home to 700,000 Iraqi refugees (equal to 10 percent of its population) and fears a flood of many more. Both Jordan and Egypt are concerned about the position of Iraq's Sunni Arabs and want constitutional reforms in Iraq to bolster the Sunni community. They also fear the return of insurgents to their countries.

The International Community

The international community beyond the United Kingdom and our other coalition partners has played a limited role in Iraq. The United Nations—acting under Security Council Resolution 1546—has a small presence in Iraq; it has assisted in holding elections, drafting the constitution, organizing the government, and building institutions. The World Bank, which has committed a limited number of resources, has one and sometimes two staff in Iraq. The European Union has a representative there.

Several U.S.-based and international nongovernmental organizations have done excellent work within Iraq, operating under great hardship. Both Iraqi and international nongovernmental organizations play an important role in reaching across sectarian lines to enhance dialogue and understanding, and several U.S.-based organizations have employed substantial resources to help Iraqis develop their democracy. However, the participation of international nongovernmental organizations is constrained by the lack of security, and their Iraqi counterparts face a cumbersome and often politicized process of registration with the government.

The United Kingdom has dedicated an extraordinary amount of resources to Iraq and has made great sacrifices. In addition to 7,200 troops, the United Kingdom has a substantial diplomatic presence, particularly in Basra and the Iraqi southeast. The United Kingdom has been an active and key player at every stage of Iraq's political development. U.K. officials told us that they remain committed to working for stability in Iraq, and will reduce their commitment of troops and resources in response to the situation on the ground.

5. Conclusions

The United States has made a massive commitment to the future of Iraq in both blood and treasure. As of December 2006, nearly 2,900 Americans have lost their lives serving in Iraq. Another 21,000 Americans have been wounded, many severely.

To date, the United States has spent roughly $400 billion on the Iraq War, and costs are running about $8 billion per month. In addition, the United States must expect significant "tail costs" to come. Caring for veterans and replacing lost equipment will run into the hundreds of billions of dollars. Estimates run as high as $2 trillion for the final cost of the U.S. involvement in Iraq.

Despite a massive effort, stability in Iraq remains elusive and the situation is deteriorating. The Iraqi government cannot now govern, sustain, and defend itself without the support of the United States. Iraqis have not been convinced that they must take responsibility for their own future. Iraq's neighbors and much of the international community have not been persuaded to play an active and constructive role in supporting Iraq. The ability of the United States to shape outcomes is diminishing. Time is running out.

B. Consequences of Continued Decline in Iraq

If the situation in Iraq continues to deteriorate, the consequences could be severe for Iraq, the United States, the region, and the world.

Continuing violence could lead toward greater chaos, and inflict greater suffering upon the Iraqi people. A collapse of Iraq's government and economy would further cripple a country already unable to meet its people's needs. Iraq's security forces could split along sectarian lines. A humanitarian catastrophe could follow as more refugees are forced to relocate across the country and the region. Ethnic cleansing could escalate. The Iraqi people could be subjected to another strongman who flexes the political and military muscle required to impose order amid anarchy. Freedoms could be lost.

Other countries in the region fear significant violence crossing their borders. Chaos in Iraq could lead those countries to intervene to protect their own interests, thereby perhaps sparking a broader regional war. Turkey could send troops into northern Iraq to prevent Kurdistan from declaring independence. Iran could send in troops to restore stability in southern Iraq and perhaps gain control of oil fields. The regional influence of Iran could rise at a time when that country is on a path to producing nuclear weapons.

Ambassadors from neighboring countries told us that they fear the distinct possibility of Sunni-Shia clashes across the Islamic world. Many expressed a fear of Shia insurrections—perhaps fomented by Iran—in Sunni-ruled states. Such a broader sectarian conflict could open a Pandora's box of problems—including the radicalization of populations, mass movements of populations, and regime changes—that might take decades to play out. If the instability in Iraq spreads to the other Gulf States, a drop in oil production and exports could lead to a sharp increase in the price of oil and thus could harm the global economy.

Terrorism could grow. As one Iraqi official told us, "Al Qaeda is now a franchise in Iraq, like McDonald's." Left unchecked, al Qaeda in Iraq could continue to incite violence between Sunnis and Shia. A chaotic Iraq could provide a still stronger base of operations for terrorists who seek to act regionally or even globally. Al Qaeda will portray any failure by the United States in Iraq as a significant victory that will be featured prominently as they recruit for their cause in the region and around the world. Ayman al-Zawahiri, deputy to Osama bin Laden, has declared Iraq a focus for al Qaeda: they will seek to expel the Americans and then spread "the jihad wave to the secular countries neighboring Iraq." A senior European official told us that failure in Iraq could incite terrorist attacks within his country.

The global standing of the United States could suffer if Iraq descends further into chaos. Iraq is a major test of, and strain on, U.S. military, diplomatic, and financial capacities. Perceived failure there could diminish America's credibility and influence in a region that is the center of the Islamic world and vital to the world's energy supply. This loss would reduce America's global influence at a time when pressing issues in North Korea, Iran, and elsewhere demand our full attention and strong U.S. leadership of international alliances. And the longer that U.S. political and military resources are tied down in Iraq, the more the chances for American failure in Afghanistan increase.

Continued problems in Iraq could lead to greater polarization within the United States. Sixty-six percent of Americans disapprove of the government's handling of the war, and more than 60 percent feel that there is no clear plan for moving forward. The November elections were largely viewed as a referendum on the progress in Iraq. Arguments about continuing to provide security and assistance to Iraq will fall on deaf ears if Americans become disillusioned with the government that the United States invested so much to create. U.S. foreign policy cannot be successfully sustained without the broad support of the American people.

Continued problems in Iraq could also lead to greater Iraqi opposition to the United States. Recent polling indicates that only 36 percent of Iraqis feel their country is heading in the right direction, and 79 percent of Iraqis have a "mostly negative" view of the influence that the United States has in their country. Sixty-one percent of Iraqis approve of attacks on U.S.-led forces. If Iraqis continue to perceive Americans as representing an occupying force, the United States could become its own worst enemy in a land it liberated from tyranny.

These and other predictions of dire consequences in Iraq and the region are by no means a certainty. Iraq has taken several positive steps since Saddam Hussein was overthrown: Iraqis restored full sovereignty, conducted open national elections, drafted a permanent constitution, ratified that constitution, and elected a new government pursuant to that constitution. Iraqis may become so sobered by the prospect of an unfolding civil war and intervention by their regional neighbors that they take the steps necessary to avert catastrophe. But at the moment, such a scenario seems implausible because the Iraqi people and their leaders have been slow to demonstrate the capacity or will to act.

C. Some Alternative Courses in Iraq

Because of the gravity of the situation in Iraq and of its consequences for Iraq, the United States, the region, and the world, the Iraq Study Group has carefully considered the full range of alternative approaches for moving forward. We recognize that there is no perfect solution and that all that have been suggested have flaws. The following are some of the more notable possibilities that we have considered.

1. Precipitate Withdrawal

Because of the importance of Iraq, the potential for catastrophe, and the role and commitments of the United States in initiating events that have led to the current situation, we believe it would be wrong for the United States to abandon the country through a precipitate withdrawal of troops and support. A premature American departure from Iraq would almost certainly produce greater sectarian violence and further deterioration of conditions, leading to a number of the adverse consequences outlined above. The near-term results would be a significant power vacuum, greater human suffering, regional destabilization, and a threat to the global economy. Al Qaeda would depict our withdrawal as a historic victory. If we leave and Iraq descends into chaos, the long-range consequences could eventually require the United States to return.

2. Staying the Course

Current U.S. policy is not working, as the level of violence in Iraq is rising and the government is not advancing national reconciliation. Making no changes in policy would simply delay the day of reckoning at a high cost. Nearly 100 Americans are dying every month. The United States is spending $2 billion a week. Our ability to respond to other international crises is constrained. A majority of the American people are soured on the war. This level of expense is not sustainable over an extended period, especially when progress is not being made. The longer the United States remains in Iraq without progress, the more resentment will grow among Iraqis who believe they are subjects of a repressive American occupation. As one U.S. official said to us, "Our leaving would make it worse. . . . The current approach without modification will not make it better."

3. More Troops for Iraq

Sustained increases in U.S. troop levels would not solve the fundamental cause of violence in Iraq, which is the absence of national reconciliation. A senior American general told us that adding U.S. troops might temporarily help limit violence in a highly localized area. However, past experience indicates that the violence would simply rekindle as soon as U.S. forces are moved to another area. As another American general told us, if the Iraqi government does not make political progress, "all the troops in the world will not provide security." Meanwhile, America's military capacity is stretched thin: we do not have the troops or equipment to make a substantial, sustained increase in our troop presence. Increased deployments to Iraq would also necessarily hamper our ability to provide adequate resources for our efforts in Afghanistan or respond to crises around the world.

4. Devolution to Three Regions

The costs associated with devolving Iraq into three semiautonomous regions with loose central control would be too high. Because Iraq's population is not neatly separated, regional boundaries cannot be easily drawn. All eighteen Iraqi provinces have mixed populations, as do Baghdad and most other major cities in Iraq. A rapid devolution could result in mass population movements, collapse of the Iraqi security forces, strengthening of militias, ethnic cleansing, destabilization of neighboring states, or attempts by neighboring states to dominate Iraqi regions. Iraqis, particularly Sunni Arabs, told us that such a division would confirm wider fears across the Arab world that the United States invaded Iraq to weaken a strong Arab state.

While such devolution is a possible consequence of continued instability in Iraq, we do not believe the United States should support this course as a policy goal or impose this outcome on the Iraqi state. If events were to move irreversibly in this direction, the United States should manage the situation to ameliorate humanitarian consequences, contain the spread of violence, and minimize regional stability. The United States should support as much as possible central control by governmental authorities in Baghdad, particularly on the question of oil revenues.

D. Achieving Our Goals

We agree with the goal of U.S. policy in Iraq, as stated by the President: an Iraq that can "govern itself, sustain itself, and defend itself." In our view, this definition entails an Iraq with a broadly representative government that maintains its territorial integrity, is at peace with its neighbors, denies terrorism a sanctuary, and doesn't brutalize its own people. Given the current situation in Iraq, achieving this goal will require much time and will depend primarily on the actions of the Iraqi people.

In our judgment, there is a new way forward for the United States to support this objective, and it will offer people of Iraq a reasonable opportunity to lead a better life than they did under Saddam Hussein. Our recommended course has shortcomings, as does each of the policy alternatives we have reviewed. We firmly believe, however, that it includes the best strategies and tactics available to us to positively influence the outcome in Iraq and the region. We believe that it could enable a responsible transition that will give the Iraqi people a chance to pursue a better future, as well as serving America's interests and values in the years ahead.

II

The Way Forward—
A New Approach

Progress in Iraq is still possible if new approaches are taken promptly by Iraq, the United States, and other countries that have a stake in the Middle East.

To attain the goals we have outlined, changes in course must be made both outside and inside Iraq. Our report offers a comprehensive strategy to build regional and international support for stability in Iraq, as it encourages the Iraqi people to assume control of their own destiny. It offers a responsible transition.

Externally, the United States should immediately begin to employ all elements of American power to construct a regional mechanism that can support, rather than retard, progress in Iraq. Internally, the Iraqi government must take the steps required to achieve national reconciliation, reduce violence, and improve the daily lives of Iraqis. Efforts to implement these external and internal strategies must begin now and must be undertaken in concert with one another.

This responsible transition can allow for a reduction in the U.S. presence in Iraq over time.

A. The External Approach: Building an International Consensus

The United States must build a new international consensus for stability in Iraq and the region.

In order to foster such consensus, the United States should embark on a robust diplomatic effort to establish an international support structure intended to stabilize Iraq and ease tensions in other countries in the region. This support structure should include every country that has an interest in averting a chaotic Iraq, including all of Iraq's neighbors—Iran and Syria among them. Despite the well-known differences between many of these countries, they all share an interest in avoiding the horrific consequences that would flow from a chaotic Iraq, particularly a humanitarian catastrophe and regional destabilization.

A reinvigorated diplomatic effort is required because it is clear that the Iraqi government cannot succeed in governing, defending, and sustaining itself by relying on U.S. military and economic support alone. Nor can the Iraqi government succeed by relying only on U.S. military support in conjunction with Iraqi military and police capabilities. Some states have been withholding commitments they could make to support Iraq's stabilization and reconstruction. Some states have been actively undermining stability in Iraq. To achieve a political solution within Iraq, a broader international support structure is needed.

1. The New Diplomatic Offensive

Iraq cannot be addressed effectively in isolation from other major regional issues, interests, and unresolved conflicts. To put it simply, all key issues in the Middle East—the Arab-Israeli conflict, Iraq, Iran, the need for political and economic reforms, and extremism and terrorism—are inextricably linked. In addition to supporting stability in Iraq, a comprehensive diplomatic offensive—the New Diplomatic Offensive—should address these key regional issues. By doing so, it would help marginalize extremists and terrorists, promote U.S. values and interests, and improve America's global image.

Under the diplomatic offensive, we propose regional and international initiatives and steps to assist the Iraqi government in achieving certain security, political, and economic milestones. Achieving these milestones will require at least the acquiescence of Iraq's neighbors, and their active and timely cooperation would be highly desirable.

The diplomatic offensive would extend beyond the primarily economic "Compact for Iraq" by also emphasizing political, diplomatic, and security issues. At the same time, it would be coordinated with the goals of the Compact for Iraq. The diplomatic offensive would also be broader and more far-reaching than the "Gulf Plus Two" efforts currently being conducted, and those efforts should be folded into and become part of the diplomatic offensive.

States included within the diplomatic offensive can play a major role in reinforcing national reconciliation efforts between Iraqi Sunnis and Shia. Such reinforcement would contribute substantially to legitimizing of the political process in Iraq. Iraq's leaders may not be able to come together unless they receive the necessary signals and support from abroad. This backing will not materialize of its own accord, and must be encouraged urgently by the United States.

In order to advance a comprehensive diplomatic solution, the Study Group recommends as follows:

RECOMMENDATION 1: The United States, working with the Iraqi government, should launch the comprehensive New Diplomatic Offensive to deal with the problems of Iraq and of the region. This new diplomatic offensive should be launched before December 31, 2006.

RECOMMENDATION 2: The goals of the diplomatic offensive as it relates to regional players should be to:

i. Support the unity and territorial integrity of Iraq.

ii. Stop destabilizing interventions and actions by Iraq's neighbors.

iii. Secure Iraq's borders, including the use of joint patrols with neighboring countries.

iv. Prevent the expansion of the instability and conflict beyond Iraq's borders.

v. Promote economic assistance, commerce, trade, political support, and, if possible, military assistance for the Iraqi government from non-neighboring Muslim nations.

vi. Energize countries to support national political reconciliation in Iraq.

vii. Validate Iraq's legitimacy by resuming diplomatic relations, where appropriate, and reestablishing embassies in Baghdad.

viii. Assist Iraq in establishing active working embassies in key capitals in the region (for example, in Riyadh, Saudi Arabia).

ix. Help Iraq reach a mutually acceptable agreement on Kirkuk.

x. Assist the Iraqi government in achieving certain security, political, and economic milestones, including better performance on issues such as national reconciliation, equitable distribution of oil revenues, and the dismantling of militias.

RECOMMENDATION 3: As a complement to the diplomatic offensive, and in addition to the Support Group discussed below, the United States and the Iraqi government should support the holding of a conference or meeting in Baghdad of the Organization of the Islamic Conference or the Arab League both to assist the Iraqi government in promoting national reconciliation in Iraq and to reestablish their diplomatic presence in Iraq.

2. The Iraq International Support Group

This new diplomatic offensive cannot be successful unless it includes the active participation of those countries that have a critical stake in preventing Iraq from falling into chaos. To encourage their participation, the United States should immediately seek the creation of the Iraq International Support Group. The Support Group should also include all countries that border Iraq as well as other key countries in the region and the world.

The Support Group would not seek to impose obligations or undertakings on the government of Iraq. Instead, the Support Group would assist Iraq in ways the government of Iraq would desire, attempting to strengthen Iraq's sovereignty—not diminish it.

It is clear to Iraq Study Group members that all of Iraq's neighbors are anxious about the situation in Iraq. They favor a unified Iraq that is strong enough to maintain its territorial integrity, but not so powerful as to threaten its neighbors. None favors the breakup of the Iraqi state. Each country in the region views the situation in Iraq through the filter of its particular set of interests. For example:

- Turkey opposes an independent or even highly autonomous Kurdistan because of its own national security considerations.

- Iran backs Shia claims and supports various Shia militias in Iraq, but it also supports other groups in order to enhance its influence and hedge its bets on possible outcomes.

- Syria, despite facilitating support for Iraqi insurgent groups, would be threatened by the impact that the breakup of Iraq would have on its own multiethnic and multiconfessional society.

- Kuwait wants to ensure that it will not once again be the victim of Iraqi irredentism and aggression.

- Saudi Arabia and Jordan share Sunni concerns over Shia ascendancy in Iraq and the region as a whole.

- The other Arab Gulf states also recognize the benefits of an outcome in Iraq that does not destabilize the region and exacerbate Shia-Sunni tensions.

- None of Iraq's neighbors—especially major countries such as Egypt, Saudi Arabia, and Israel—see it in their interest for the situation in Iraq to lead to aggrandized regional influence by Iran. Indeed, they may take active steps to limit Iran's influence, steps that could lead to an intraregional conflict.

Left to their own devices, these governments will tend to reinforce ethnic, sectarian, and political divisions within Iraqi society. But if the Support Group takes a systematic and active approach toward considering the concerns of each country, we believe that each can be encouraged to play a positive role in Iraq and the region.

SAUDI ARABIA. Saudi Arabia's agreement not to intervene with assistance to Sunni Arab Iraqis could be an essential quid pro quo for similar forbearance on the part of other neighbors, especially Iran. The Saudis could use their Islamic credentials to help reconcile differences between Iraqi factions and build broader support in the Islamic world for a stabilization agreement, as their recent hosting of a meeting of Islamic religious leaders in Mecca suggests. If the government in Baghdad pursues a path of national reconciliation with the Sunnis, the Saudis could help Iraq confront and eliminate al Qaeda in Iraq. They could also cancel the Iraqi debt owed them. In addition, the Saudis might be helpful in persuading the Syrians to cooperate.

TURKEY.   As a major Sunni Muslim country on Iraq's borders, Turkey can be a partner in supporting the national reconciliation process in Iraq. Such efforts can be particularly helpful given Turkey's interest in Kurdistan remaining an integral part of a unified Iraq and its interest in preventing a safe haven for Kurdish terrorists (the PKK).

EGYPT.   Because of its important role in the Arab world, Egypt should be encouraged to foster the national reconciliation process in Iraq with a focus on getting the Sunnis to participate. At the same time, Egypt has the means, and indeed has offered, to train groups of Iraqi military and security forces in Egypt on a rotational basis.

JORDAN.   Jordan, like Egypt, can help in the national reconciliation process in Iraq with the Sunnis. It too has the professional capability to train and equip Iraqi military and security forces.

RECOMMENDATION 4: As an instrument of the New Diplomatic Offensive, an Iraq International Support Group should be organized immediately following the launch of the New Diplomatic Offensive.

RECOMMENDATION 5: The Support Group should consist of Iraq and all the states bordering Iraq, including Iran and Syria; the key regional states, including Egypt and the Gulf States; the five permanent members of the United Nations Security Council; the European Union; and, of course, Iraq itself. Other countries—for instance, Germany, Japan and South Korea—that might be willing to contribute to resolving political, diplomatic, and security problems affecting Iraq could also become members.

RECOMMENDATION 6: *The New Diplomatic Offensive and the work of the Support Group should be carried out with urgency, and should be conducted by and organized at the level of foreign minister or above. The Secretary of State, if not the President, should lead the U.S. effort. That effort should be both bilateral and multilateral, as circumstances require.*

RECOMMENDATION 7: *The Support Group should call on the participation of the office of the United Nations Secretary-General in its work. The United Nations Secretary-General should designate a Special Envoy as his representative.*

RECOMMENDATION 8: *The Support Group, as part of the New Diplomatic Offensive, should develop specific approaches to neighboring countries that take into account the interests, perspectives, and potential contributions as suggested above.*

3. Dealing with Iran and Syria

Dealing with Iran and Syria is controversial. Nevertheless, it is our view that in diplomacy, a nation can and should engage its adversaries and enemies to try to resolve conflicts and differences consistent with its own interests. Accordingly, the Support Group should actively engage Iran and Syria in its diplomatic dialogue, without preconditions.

The Study Group recognizes that U.S. relationships with Iran and Syria involve difficult issues that must be resolved. Diplomatic talks should be extensive and substantive, and they will require a balancing of interests. The United States has diplomatic, economic, and military disincentives available in approaches to both Iran and Syria. However, the United States should also consider incentives to try to engage them constructively, much as it did successfully with Libya.

Some of the possible incentives to Iran, Syria, or both include:

i. An Iraq that does not disintegrate and destabilize its neighbors and the region.

ii. The continuing role of the United States in preventing the Taliban from destabilizing Afghanistan.

iii. Accession to international organizations, including the World Trade Organization.

iv. Prospects for enhanced diplomatic relations with the United States.

v. The prospect of a U.S. policy that emphasizes political and economic reforms instead of (as Iran now perceives it) advocating regime change.

vi. Prospects for a real, complete, and secure peace to be negotiated between Israel and Syria, with U.S. involvement as part of a broader initiative on Arab-Israeli peace as outlined below.

RECOMMENDATION 9: *Under the aegis of the New Diplomatic Offensive and the Support Group, the United States should engage directly with Iran and Syria in order to try to obtain their commitment to constructive policies toward Iraq and other regional issues. In engaging Syria and Iran, the*

United States should consider incentives, as well as disincentives, in seeking constructive results.

IRAN.   Engaging Iran is problematic, especially given the state of the U.S.-Iranian relationship. Yet the United States and Iran cooperated in Afghanistan, and both sides should explore whether this model can be replicated in the case of Iraq.

Although Iran sees it in its interest to have the United States bogged down in Iraq, Iran's interests would not be served by a failure of U.S. policy in Iraq that led to chaos and the territorial disintegration of the Iraqi state. Iran's population is slightly more than 50 percent Persian, but it has a large Azeri minority (24 percent of the population) as well as Kurdish and Arab minorities. Worst-case scenarios in Iraq could inflame sectarian tensions within Iran, with serious consequences for Iranian national security interests.

Our limited contacts with Iran's government lead us to believe that its leaders are likely to say they will not participate in diplomatic efforts to support stability in Iraq. They attribute this reluctance to their belief that the United States seeks regime change in Iran.

Nevertheless, as one of Iraq's neighbors Iran should be asked to assume its responsibility to participate in the Support Group. An Iranian refusal to do so would demonstrate to Iraq and the rest of the world Iran's rejectionist attitude and approach, which could lead to its isolation. Further, Iran's refusal to cooperate on this matter would diminish its prospects of engaging with the United States in the broader dialogue it seeks.

RECOMMENDATION 10: The issue of Iran's nuclear programs should continue to be dealt with by the United Nations Security Council and its five permanent members (i.e., the

*United States, United Kingdom, France, Russia, and China)
plus Germany.*

RECOMMENDATION 11: *Diplomatic efforts within the
Support Group should seek to persuade Iran that it should
take specific steps to improve the situation in Iraq.*

Among steps Iran could usefully take are the following:

- Iran should stem the flow of equipment, technology, and
  training to any group resorting to violence in Iraq.

- Iran should make clear its support for the territorial integrity
  of Iraq as a unified state, as well as its respect for the sovereignty of Iraq and its government.

- Iran can use its influence, especially over Shia groups in Iraq,
  to encourage national reconciliation.

- Iran can also, in the right circumstances, help in the economic reconstruction of Iraq.

SYRIA.   Although the U.S.-Syrian relationship is at a low point,
both countries have important interests in the region that could
be enhanced if they were able to establish some common
ground on how to move forward. This approach worked effectively in the early 1990s. In this context, Syria's national interests
in the Arab-Israeli dispute are important and can be brought
into play.

    Syria can make a major contribution to Iraq's stability in
several ways. Accordingly, the Study Group recommends the
following:

RECOMMENDATION 12: The United States and the Support Group should encourage and persuade Syria of the merit of such contributions as the following:

- *Syria can control its border with Iraq to the maximum extent possible and work together with Iraqis on joint patrols on the border. Doing so will help stem the flow of funding, insurgents, and terrorists in and out of Iraq.*

- *Syria can establish hotlines to exchange information with the Iraqis.*

- *Syria can increase its political and economic cooperation with Iraq.*

4. The Wider Regional Context

The United States will not be able to achieve its goals in the Middle East unless the United States deals directly with the Arab-Israeli conflict.

There must be a renewed and sustained commitment by the United States to a comprehensive Arab-Israeli peace on all fronts: Lebanon, Syria, and President Bush's June 2002 commitment to a two-state solution for Israel and Palestine. This commitment must include direct talks with, by, and between Israel, Lebanon, Palestinians (those who accept Israel's right to exist), and particularly Syria—which is the principal transit point for shipments of weapons to Hezbollah, and which supports radical Palestinian groups.

The United States does its ally Israel no favors in avoiding direct involvement to solve the Arab-Israeli conflict. For several reasons, we should act boldly:

- There is no military solution to this conflict.

- The vast majority of the Israeli body politic is tired of being a nation perpetually at war.

- No American administration—Democratic or Republican—will ever abandon Israel.

- Political engagement and dialogue are essential in the Arab-Israeli dispute because it is an axiom that when the political process breaks down there will be violence on the ground.

- The only basis on which peace can be achieved is that set forth in UN Security Council Resolutions 242 and 338 and in the principle of "land for peace."

- The only lasting and secure peace will be a negotiated peace such as Israel has achieved with Egypt and Jordan.

This effort would strongly support moderate Arab governments in the region, especially the democratically elected government of Lebanon, and the Palestinian Authority under President Mahmoud Abbas.

RECOMMENDATION 13: There must be a renewed and sustained commitment by the United States to a comprehensive Arab-Israeli peace on all fronts: Lebanon and Syria, and President Bush's June 2002 commitment to a two-state solution for Israel and Palestine.

RECOMMENDATION 14: This effort should include—as soon as possible—the unconditional calling and holding of meetings, under the auspices of the United States or the Quartet (i.e., the United States, Russia, European Union, and the United Nations), between Israel and Lebanon and Syria on the one hand, and Israel and Palestinians (who acknowledge Israel's right to exist) on the other. The purpose of these meetings would be to negotiate peace as was done at the Madrid Conference in 1991, and on two separate tracks— one Syrian/Lebanese, and the other Palestinian.

RECOMMENDATION 15: Concerning Syria, some elements of that negotiated peace should be:

- Syria's full adherence to UN Security Council Resolution 1701 of August 2006, which provides the framework for Lebanon to regain sovereign control over its territory.

- Syria's full cooperation with all investigations into political assassinations in Lebanon, especially those of Rafik Hariri and Pierre Gemayel.

- A verifiable cessation of Syrian aid to Hezbollah and the use of Syrian territory for transshipment of Iranian weapons and aid to Hezbollah. (This step would do much to solve Israel's problem with Hezbollah.)

- Syria's use of its influence with Hamas and Hezbollah for the release of the captured Israeli Defense Force soldiers.

- A verifiable cessation of Syrian efforts to undermine the democratically elected government of Lebanon.

- *A verifiable cessation of arms shipments from or transiting through Syria for Hamas and other radical Palestinian groups.*

- *A Syrian commitment to help obtain from Hamas an acknowledgment of Israel's right to exist.*

- *Greater Syrian efforts to seal its border with Iraq.*

RECOMMENDATION 16: In exchange for these actions and in the context of a full and secure peace agreement, the Israelis should return the Golan Heights, with a U.S. security guarantee for Israel that could include an international force on the border, including U.S. troops if requested by both parties.

RECOMMENDATION 17: Concerning the Palestinian issue, elements of that negotiated peace should include:

- *Adherence to UN Security Council Resolutions 242 and 338 and to the principle of land for peace, which are the only bases for achieving peace.*

- *Strong support for Palestinian President Mahmoud Abbas and the Palestinian Authority to take the lead in preparing the way for negotiations with Israel.*

- *A major effort to move from the current hostilities by consolidating the cease-fire reached between the Palestinians and the Israelis in November 2006.*

- *Support for a Palestinian national unity government.*

- *Sustainable negotiations leading to a final peace settlement along the lines of President Bush's two-state solution, which would address the key final status issues of borders, settlements, Jerusalem, the right of return, and the end of conflict.*

Afghanistan

At the same time, we must not lose sight of the importance of the situation inside Afghanistan and the renewed threat posed by the Taliban. Afghanistan's borders are porous. If the Taliban were to control more of Afghanistan, it could provide al Qaeda the political space to conduct terrorist operations. This development would destabilize the region and have national security implications for the United States and other countries around the world. Also, the significant increase in poppy production in Afghanistan fuels the illegal drug trade and narco-terrorism.

The huge focus of U.S. political, military, and economic support on Iraq has necessarily diverted attention from Afghanistan. As the United States develops its approach toward Iraq and the Middle East, it must also give priority to the situation in Afghanistan. Doing so may require increased political, security, and military measures.

RECOMMENDATION 18: *It is critical for the United States to provide additional political, economic, and military support for Afghanistan, including resources that might become available as combat forces are moved from Iraq.*

B. The Internal Approach:
Helping Iraqis Help Themselves

The New Diplomatic Offensive will provide the proper external environment and support for the difficult internal steps that the Iraqi government must take to promote national reconciliation, establish security, and make progress on governance.

The most important issues facing Iraq's future are now the responsibility of Iraq's elected leaders. Because of the security and assistance it provides, the United States has a significant role to play. Yet only the government and people of Iraq can make and sustain certain decisions critical to Iraq's future.

1. Performance on Milestones

The United States should work closely with Iraq's leaders to support the achievement of specific objectives—or milestones—on national reconciliation, security, and governance. Miracles cannot be expected, but the people of Iraq have the right to expect action and progress. The Iraqi government needs to show its own citizens—and the citizens of the United States and other countries—that it deserves continued support.

The U.S. government must make clear that it expects action by the Iraqi government to make substantial progress toward these milestones. Such a message can be sent only at the level of our national leaders, and only in person, during direct consultation.

As President Bush's meeting with Prime Minister Maliki in Amman, Jordan demonstrates, it is important for the President to remain in close and frequent contact with the Iraqi leadership. There is no substitute for sustained dialogue at the highest levels of government.

During these high-level exchanges, the United States should lay out an agenda for continued support to help Iraq achieve milestones, as well as underscoring the consequences if Iraq does not act. It should be unambiguous that continued U.S. political, military, and economic support for Iraq depends on the Iraqi government's demonstrating political will and making substantial progress toward the achievement of milestones on national reconciliation, security, and governance. The transfer of command and control over Iraqi security forces units from the United States to Iraq should be influenced by Iraq's performance on milestones.

The United States should also signal that it is seeking broad international support for Iraq on behalf of achieving these milestones. The United States can begin to shape a positive climate for its diplomatic efforts, internationally and within Iraq, through public statements by President Bush that reject the notion that the United States seeks to control Iraq's oil, or seeks permanent military bases within Iraq. However, the United States could consider a request from Iraq for temporary bases.

RECOMMENDATION 19: The President and the leadership of his national security team should remain in close and fre-

quent contact with the Iraqi leadership. These contacts must convey a clear message: there must be action by the Iraqi government to make substantial progress toward the achievement of milestones. In public diplomacy, the President should convey as much detail as possible about the substance of these exchanges in order to keep the American people, the Iraqi people, and the countries in the region well informed.

RECOMMENDATION 20: *If the Iraqi government demonstrates political will and makes substantial progress toward the achievement of milestones on national reconciliation, security, and governance, the United States should make clear its willingness to continue training, assistance, and support for Iraq's security forces, and to continue political, military, and economic support for the Iraqi government. As Iraq becomes more capable of governing, defending, and sustaining itself, the U.S. military and civilian presence in Iraq can be reduced.*

RECOMMENDATION 21: *If the Iraqi government does not make substantial progress toward the achievement of milestones on national reconciliation, security, and governance, the United States should reduce its political, military, or economic support for the Iraqi government.*

RECOMMENDATION 22: *The President should state that the United States does not seek permanent military bases in Iraq. If the Iraqi government were to request a temporary base or bases, then the U.S. government could consider that request as it would in the case of any other government.*

RECOMMENDATION 23: *The President should restate that the United States does not seek to control Iraq's oil.*

Milestones for Iraq

The government of Iraq understands that dramatic steps are necessary to avert a downward spiral and make progress. Prime Minister Maliki has worked closely in consultation with the United States and has put forward the following milestones in the key areas of national reconciliation, security and governance:

NATIONAL RECONCILIATION

By the end of 2006–early 2007:

- ➤ Approval of the Provincial Election Law and setting an election date

- ➤ Approval of the Petroleum Law

- ➤ Approval of the De-Baathification Law

- ➤ Approval of the Militia Law

By March 2007:

- ➤ A referendum on constitutional amendments (if it is necessary)

By May 2007:

- ➤ Completion of Militia Law implementation

- ➤ Approval of amnesty agreement

- ➤ Completion of reconciliation efforts

By June 2007:

➤ Provincial elections

SECURITY (pending joint U.S.-Iraqi review)

By the end of 2006:

➤ Iraqi increase of 2007 security spending over 2006 levels

By April 2007:

➤ Iraqi control of the Army

By September 2007:

➤ Iraqi control of provinces

By December 2007:

➤ Iraqi security self-reliance (with U.S. support)

GOVERNANCE

By the end of 2006:

➤ The Central Bank of Iraq will raise interest rates to 20 percent and appreciate the Iraqi dinar by 10 percent to combat accelerating inflation.

➤ Iraq will continue increasing domestic prices for refined petroleum products and sell imported fuel at market prices.

RECOMMENDATION 24: The contemplated completion dates of the end of 2006 or early 2007 for some milestones may not be realistic. These should be completed by the first quarter of 2007.

RECOMMENDATION 25: These milestones are a good start. The United States should consult closely with the Iraqi government and develop additional milestones in three areas: national reconciliation, security, and improving government services affecting the daily lives of Iraqis. As with the current milestones, these additional milestones should be tied to calendar dates to the fullest extent possible.

2. National Reconciliation

National reconciliation is essential to reduce further violence and maintain the unity of Iraq.

U.S. forces can help provide stability for a time to enable Iraqi leaders to negotiate political solutions, but they cannot stop the violence—or even contain it—if there is no underlying political agreement among Iraqis about the future of their country.

The Iraqi government must send a clear signal to Sunnis that there is a place for them in national life. The government needs to act now, to give a signal of hope. Unless Sunnis believe they can get a fair deal in Iraq through the political process, there is no prospect that the insurgency will end. To strike this fair deal, the Iraqi government and the Iraqi people must address several issues that are critical to the success of national reconciliation and thus to the future of Iraq.

Steps for Iraq to Take on Behalf of
National Reconciliation

RECOMMENDATION 26: Constitution review. *Review of the constitution is essential to national reconciliation and should be pursued on an urgent basis. The United Nations has expertise in this field, and should play a role in this process.*

RECOMMENDATION 27: De-Baathification. *Political reconciliation requires the reintegration of Baathists and Arab nationalists into national life, with the leading figures of Saddam Hussein's regime excluded. The United States should encourage the return of qualified Iraqi professionals—Sunni or Shia, nationalist or ex-Baathist, Kurd or Turkmen or Christian or Arab—into the government.*

RECOMMENDATION 28: Oil revenue sharing. *Oil revenues should accrue to the central government and be shared on the basis of population. No formula that gives control over revenues from future fields to the regions or gives control of oil fields to the regions is compatible with national reconciliation.*

RECOMMENDATION 29: Provincial elections. *Provincial elections should be held at the earliest possible date. Under the constitution, new provincial elections should have been held already. They are necessary to restore representative government.*

RECOMMENDATION 30: Kirkuk. *Given the very dangerous situation in Kirkuk, international arbitration is necessary to avert communal violence. Kirkuk's mix of Kurdish, Arab,* *and Turkmen populations could make it a powder keg. A referendum on the future of Kirkuk (as required by the Iraqi Constitution before the end of 2007) would be explosive and should be delayed. This issue should be placed on the agenda of the International Iraq Support Group as part of the New Diplomatic Offensive.*

RECOMMENDATION 31: Amnesty. Amnesty proposals must be far-reaching. Any successful effort at national reconciliation must involve those in the government finding ways and means to reconcile with former bitter enemies.

RECOMMENDATION 32: Minorities. The rights of women and the rights of all minority communities in Iraq, including Turkmen, Chaldeans, Assyrians, Yazidis, Sabeans, and Armenians, must be protected.

RECOMMENDATION 33: Civil society. The Iraqi government should stop using the process of registering nongovernmental organizations as a tool for politicizing or stopping their activities. Registration should be solely an administrative act, not an occasion for government censorship and interference.

*Steps for the United States to Take on Behalf of
National Reconciliation*

The United States can take several steps to assist in Iraq's reconciliation process.

The presence of U.S. forces in Iraq is a key topic of interest in a national reconciliation dialogue. The point is not for the

United States to set timetables or deadlines for withdrawal, an approach that we oppose. The point is for the United States and Iraq to make clear their shared interest in the orderly departure of U.S. forces as Iraqi forces take on the security mission. A successful national reconciliation dialogue will advance that departure date.

RECOMMENDATION 34: The question of the future U.S. force presence must be on the table for discussion as the national reconciliation dialogue takes place. Its inclusion will increase the likelihood of participation by insurgents and militia leaders, and thereby increase the possibilities for success.

Violence cannot end unless dialogue begins, and the dialogue must involve those who wield power, not simply those who hold political office. The United States must try to talk directly to Grand Ayatollah Sistani and must consider appointing a high-level American Shia Muslim to serve as an emissary to him. The United States must also try to talk directly to Moqtada al-Sadr, to militia leaders, and to insurgent leaders. The United Nations can help facilitate contacts.

RECOMMENDATION 35: The United States must make active efforts to engage all parties in Iraq, with the exception of al Qaeda. The United States must find a way to talk to Grand Ayatollah Sistani, Moqtada al-Sadr, and militia and insurgent leaders.

The very focus on sectarian identity that endangers Iraq also presents opportunities to seek broader support for a national reconciliation dialogue. Working with Iraqi leaders, the international community and religious leaders can play an important role in fostering dialogue and reconciliation across the sectarian divide. The United States should actively encourage the constructive participation of all who can take part in advancing national reconciliation within Iraq.

RECOMMENDATION 36: The United States should encourage dialogue between sectarian communities, as outlined in the New Diplomatic Offensive above. It should press religious leaders inside and outside Iraq to speak out on behalf of peace and reconciliation.

Finally, amnesty proposals from the Iraqi government are an important incentive in reconciliation talks and they need to be generous. Amnesty proposals to once-bitter enemies will be difficult for the United States to accept, just as they will be difficult for the Iraqis to make. Yet amnesty is an issue to be grappled with by the Iraqis, not by Americans. Despite being politically unpopular—in the United States as well as in Iraq—amnesty is essential if progress is to take place. Iraqi leaders need to be certain that they have U.S. support as they move forward with this critical element of national reconciliation.

RECOMMENDATION 37: Iraqi amnesty proposals must not be undercut in Washington by either the executive or the legislative branch.

Militias and National Reconciliation

The use of force by the government of Iraq is appropriate and necessary to stop militias that act as death squads or use violence against institutions of the state. However, solving the problem of militias requires national reconciliation.

Dealing with Iraq's militias will require long-term attention, and substantial funding will be needed to disarm, demobilize, and reintegrate militia members into civilian society. Around the world, this process of transitioning members of irregular military forces from civil conflict to new lives once a peace settlement takes hold is familiar. The disarmament, demobilization, and reintegration of militias depends on national reconciliation and on confidence-building measures among the parties to that reconciliation.

Both the United Nations and expert and experienced nongovernmental organizations, especially the International Organization for Migration, must be on the ground with appropriate personnel months before any program to disarm, demobilize, and reintegrate militia members begins. Because the United States is a party to the conflict, the U.S. military should not be involved in implementing such a program. Yet U.S. financial and technical support is crucial.

RECOMMENDATION 38: The United States should support the presence of neutral international experts as advisors to the Iraqi government on the processes of disarmament, demobilization, and reintegration.

RECOMMENDATION 39: The United States should provide financial and technical support and establish a single office in Iraq to coordinate assistance to the Iraqi government and its expert advisors to aid a program to disarm, demobilize, and reintegrate militia members.

3. Security and Military Forces

A Military Strategy for Iraq

There is no action the American military can take that, by itself, can bring about success in Iraq. But there are actions that the U.S. and Iraqi governments, working together, can and should take to increase the probability of avoiding disaster there, and increase the chance of success.

The Iraqi government should accelerate the urgently needed national reconciliation program to which it has already committed. And it should accelerate assuming responsibility for Iraqi security by increasing the number and quality of Iraqi Army brigades. As the Iraqi Army increases in size and capability, the Iraqi government should be able to take real responsibility for governance.

While this process is under way, and to facilitate it, the United States should significantly increase the number of U.S. military personnel, including combat troops, imbedded in and supporting Iraqi Army units. As these actions proceed, we could begin to move combat forces out of Iraq. The primary mission of U.S. forces in Iraq should evolve to one of supporting the Iraqi army, which would take over primary responsibility for combat operations. We should continue to maintain support forces, rapid-reaction forces, special operations forces, intelligence units, search-and-rescue units, and force protection units.

While the size and composition of the Iraqi Army is ultimately a matter for the Iraqi government to determine, we should be firm on the urgent near-term need for significant additional trained Army brigades, since this is the key to Iraqis taking over full responsibility for their own security, which they want to do and which we need them to do. It is clear that they will still need security assistance from the United States for some time to come as they work to achieve political and security changes.

One of the most important elements of our support would be the imbedding of substantially more U.S. military personnel in all Iraqi Army battalions and brigades, as well as within Iraqi companies. U.S. personnel would provide advice, combat assistance, and staff assistance. The training of Iraqi units by the United States has improved and should continue for the coming year. In addition to this training, Iraqi combat units need supervised on-the-job training as they move to field operations. This on-the-job training could be best done by imbedding more U.S. military personnel in Iraqi deployed units. The number of imbedded personnel would be based on the recommendation of our military commanders in Iraq, but it should be large enough to accelerate the development of a real combat capability in Iraqi Army units. Such a mission could involve 10,000 to 20,000 American troops instead of the 3,000 to 4,000 now in this role. This increase in imbedded troops could be carried out without an aggregate increase over time in the total number of troops in Iraq by making a corresponding decrease in troops assigned to U.S. combat brigades.

Another mission of the U.S. military would be to assist Iraqi deployed brigades with intelligence, transportation, air support, and logistics support, as well as providing some key equipment.

A vital mission of the U.S. military would be to maintain rapid-reaction teams and special operations teams. These teams would be available to undertake strike missions against al Qaeda in Iraq when the opportunity arises, as well as for other missions considered vital by the U.S. commander in Iraq.

The performance of the Iraqi Army could also be significantly improved if it had improved equipment. One source could be equipment left behind by departing U.S. units. The quickest and most effective way for the Iraqi Army to get the bulk of their equipment would be through our Foreign Military Sales program, which they have already begun to use.

While these efforts are building up, and as additional Iraqi brigades are being deployed, U.S. combat brigades could begin to move out of Iraq. By the first quarter of 2008, subject to unexpected developments in the security situation on the ground, all combat brigades not necessary for force protection could be out of Iraq. At that time, U.S. combat forces in Iraq could be deployed only in units embedded with Iraqi forces, in rapid-reaction and special operations teams, and in training, equipping, advising, force protection, and search and rescue. Intelligence and support efforts would continue. Even after the United States has moved all combat brigades out of Iraq, we would maintain a considerable military presence in the region, with our still significant force in Iraq and with our powerful air, ground, and naval deployments in Kuwait, Bahrain, and Qatar, as well as an increased presence in Afghanistan. These forces would be sufficiently robust to permit the United States, working with the Iraqi government, to accomplish four missions:

- Provide political reassurance to the Iraqi government in order to avoid its collapse and the disintegration of the country.

- Fight al Qaeda and other terrorist organizations in Iraq using special operations teams.

- Train, equip, and support the Iraqi security forces.

- Deter even more destructive interference in Iraq by Syria and Iran.

Because of the importance of Iraq to our regional security goals and to our ongoing fight against al Qaeda, we considered proposals to make a substantial increase (100,000 to 200,000) in the number of U.S. troops in Iraq. We rejected this course because we do not believe that the needed levels are available for a sustained deployment. Further, adding more American troops could conceivably worsen those aspects of the security problem that are fed by the view that the U.S. presence is intended to be a long-term "occupation." We could, however, support a short-term redeployment or surge of American combat forces to stabilize Baghdad, or to speed up the training and equipping mission, if the U.S. commander in Iraq determines that such steps would be effective.

We also rejected the immediate withdrawal of our troops, because we believe that so much is at stake.

We believe that our recommended actions will give the Iraqi Army the support it needs to have a reasonable chance to take responsibility for Iraq's security. Given the ongoing deterioration in the security situation, it is urgent to move as quickly as possible to have that security role taken over by Iraqi security forces.

The United States should not make an open-ended commitment to keep large numbers of American troops deployed in Iraq for three compelling reasons.

First, and most importantly, the United States faces other security dangers in the world, and a continuing Iraqi commitment of American ground forces at present levels will leave no reserve available to meet other contingencies. On September

7, 2006, General James Jones, our NATO commander, called for more troops in Afghanistan, where U.S. and NATO forces are fighting a resurgence of al Qaeda and Taliban forces. The United States should respond positively to that request, and be prepared for other security contingencies, including those in Iran and North Korea.

Second, the long-term commitment of American ground forces to Iraq at current levels is adversely affecting Army readiness, with less than a third of the Army units currently at high readiness levels. The Army is unlikely to be able to meet the next rotation of troops in Iraq without undesirable changes in its deployment practices. The Army is now considering breaking its compact with the National Guard and Reserves that limits the number of years that these citizen-soldiers can be deployed. Behind this short-term strain is the longer-term risk that the ground forces will be impaired in ways that will take years to reverse.

And finally, an open-ended commitment of American forces would not provide the Iraqi government the incentive it needs to take the political actions that give Iraq the best chance of quelling sectarian violence. In the absence of such an incentive, the Iraqi government might continue to delay taking those difficult actions.

While it is clear that the presence of U.S. troops in Iraq is moderating the violence, there is little evidence that the long-term deployment of U.S. troops by itself has led or will lead to fundamental improvements in the security situation. It is important to recognize that there are no risk-free alternatives available to the United States at this time. Reducing our combat troop commitments in Iraq, whenever that occurs, undeniably creates risks, but leaving those forces tied down in Iraq indefinitely creates its own set of security risks.

RECOMMENDATION 40: The United States should not make an open-ended commitment to keep large numbers of American troops deployed in Iraq.

RECOMMENDATION 41: The United States must make it clear to the Iraqi government that the United States could carry out its plans, including planned redeployments, even if Iraq does not implement its planned changes. America's other security needs and the future of our military cannot be made hostage to the actions or inactions of the Iraqi government.

RECOMMENDATION 42: We should seek to complete the training and equipping mission by the first quarter of 2008, as stated by General George Casey on October 24, 2006.

RECOMMENDATION 43: Military priorities in Iraq must change, with the highest priority given to the training, equipping, advising, and support mission and to counterterrorism operations.

RECOMMENDATION 44: The most highly qualified U.S. officers and military personnel should be assigned to the imbedded teams, and American teams should be present with Iraqi units down to the company level. The U.S. military should establish suitable career-enhancing incentives for these officers and personnel.

RECOMMENDATION 45: The United States should support more and better equipment for the Iraqi Army by encouraging the Iraqi government to accelerate its Foreign Military Sales requests and, as American combat brigades *move out of Iraq, by leaving behind some American equipment for Iraqi forces.*

Restoring the U.S. Military

We recognize that there are other results of the war in Iraq that have great consequence for our nation. One consequence has been the stress and uncertainty imposed on our military—the most professional and proficient military in history. The United States will need its military to protect U.S. security regardless of what happens in Iraq. We therefore considered how to limit the adverse consequences of the strain imposed on our military by the Iraq war.

U.S. military forces, especially our ground forces, have been stretched nearly to the breaking point by the repeated deployments in Iraq, with attendant casualties (almost 3,000 dead and more than 21,000 wounded), greater difficulty in recruiting, and accelerated wear on equipment.

Additionally, the defense budget as a whole is in danger of disarray, as supplemental funding winds down and reset costs become clear. It will be a major challenge to meet ongoing requirements for other current and future security threats that need to be accommodated together with spending for operations and maintenance, reset, personnel, and benefits for active duty and retired personnel. Restoring the capability of our military forces should be a high priority for the United States at this time.

The U.S. military has a long tradition of strong partnership between the civilian leadership of the Department of Defense and the uniformed services. Both have long benefited from a relationship in which the civilian leadership exercises control with the advantage of fully candid professional advice, and the military serves loyally with the understanding that its advice has been heard and valued. That tradition has frayed, and civil-military relations need to be repaired.

RECOMMENDATION 46: The new Secretary of Defense should make every effort to build healthy civil-military relations, by creating an environment in which the senior military feel free to offer independent advice not only to the civilian leadership in the Pentagon but also to the President and the National Security Council, as envisioned in the Goldwater-Nichols legislation.

RECOMMENDATION 47: As redeployment proceeds, the Pentagon leadership should emphasize training and education programs for the forces that have returned to the continental United States in order to "reset" the force and restore the U.S. military to a high level of readiness for global contingencies.

RECOMMENDATION 48: As equipment returns to the United States, Congress should appropriate sufficient funds to restore the equipment to full functionality over the next five years.

RECOMMENDATION 49: The administration, in full consultation with the relevant committees of Congress, should assess the full future budgetary impact of the war in Iraq and its potential impact on the future readiness of the force, the ability to recruit and retain high-quality personnel, needed investments in procurement and in research and development, and the budgets of other U.S. government agencies involved in the stability and reconstruction effort.

4. Police and Criminal Justice

The problems in the Iraqi police and criminal justice system are profound.

The ethos and training of Iraqi police forces must support the mission to "protect and serve" all Iraqis. Today, far too many Iraqi police do not embrace that mission, in part because of problems in how reforms were organized and implemented by the Iraqi and U.S. governments.

Recommended Iraqi Actions

Within Iraq, the failure of the police to restore order and prevent militia infiltration is due, in part, to the poor organization of Iraq's component police forces: the Iraqi National Police, the Iraqi Border Police, and the Iraqi Police Service.

The Iraqi National Police pursue a mission that is more military than domestic in nature—involving commando-style operations—and is thus ill-suited to the Ministry of the Interior. The more natural home for the National Police is within the Ministry of Defense, which should be the authority for counterinsurgency operations and heavily armed forces. Though depriving the Ministry of the Interior of operational forces, this move will place the Iraqi National Police under better and more rigorous Iraqi and U.S. supervision and will enable these units to better perform their counterinsurgency mission.

RECOMMENDATION 50: *The entire Iraqi National Police should be transferred to the Ministry of Defense, where the police commando units will become part of the new Iraqi Army.*

Similarly, the Iraqi Border Police are charged with a role that bears little resemblance to ordinary policing, especially in light of the current flow of foreign fighters, insurgents, and weaponry across Iraq's borders and the need for joint patrols of the border with foreign militaries. Thus the natural home for the Border Police is within the Ministry of Defense, which should be the authority for controlling Iraq's borders.

RECOMMENDATION 51: *The entire Iraqi Border Police should be transferred to the Ministry of Defense, which would have total responsibility for border control and external security.*

The Iraqi Police Service, which operates in the provinces and provides local policing, needs to become a true police force. It needs legal authority, training, and equipment to control crime and protect Iraqi citizens. Accomplishing those goals will not be easy, and the presence of American advisors will be required to help the Iraqis determine a new role for the police.

RECOMMENDATION 52: *The Iraqi Police Service should be given greater responsibility to conduct criminal investigations and should expand its cooperation with other elements in the Iraqi judicial system in order to better control crime and protect Iraqi civilians.*

In order to more effectively administer the Iraqi Police Service, the Ministry of the Interior needs to undertake substantial reforms to purge bad elements and highlight best practices. Once the ministry begins to function effectively, it can exert a positive influence over the provinces and take back some of the authority that was lost to local governments through decentralization. To reduce corruption and militia infiltration, the Ministry of the Interior should take authority from the local governments for the handling of policing funds. Doing so will improve accountability and organizational discipline, limit the authority of provincial police officials, and identify police officers with the central government.

RECOMMENDATION 53: The Iraqi Ministry of the Interior should undergo a process of organizational transformation, including efforts to expand the capability and reach of the current major crime unit (or Criminal Investigation Division) and to exert more authority over local police forces. The sole authority to pay police salaries and disburse financial support to local police should be transferred to the Ministry of the Interior.

Finally, there is no alternative to bringing the Facilities Protection Service under the control of the Iraqi Ministry of the Interior. Simply disbanding these units is not an option, as the members will take their weapons and become full-time militiamen or insurgents. All should be brought under the authority of a reformed Ministry of the Interior. They will need to be vetted, retrained, and closely supervised. Those who are no longer part of the Facilities Protection Service need to participate in a disarmament, demobilization, and reintegration program (outlined above).

RECOMMENDATION 54: The Iraqi Ministry of the Interior should proceed with current efforts to identify, register, and control the Facilities Protection Service.

The Way Forward—A New Approach

U.S. Actions

The Iraqi criminal justice system is weak, and the U.S. training mission has been hindered by a lack of clarity and capacity. It has not always been clear who is in charge of the police training mission, and the U.S. military lacks expertise in certain areas pertaining to police and the rule of law. The United States has been more successful in training the Iraqi Army than it has the police. The U.S. Department of Justice has the expertise and capacity to carry out the police training mission. The U.S. Department of Defense is already bearing too much of the burden in Iraq. Meanwhile, the pool of expertise in the United States on policing and the rule of law has been underutilized.

The United States should adjust its training mission in Iraq to match the recommended changes in the Iraqi government—the movement of the National and Border Police to the Ministry of Defense and the new emphasis on the Iraqi Police Service within the Ministry of the Interior. To reflect the reorganization, the Department of Defense would continue to train the Iraqi National and Border Police, and the Department of Justice would become responsible for training the Iraqi Police Service.

RECOMMENDATION 55: *The U.S. Department of Defense should continue its mission to train the Iraqi National Police and the Iraqi Border Police, which should be placed within the Iraqi Ministry of Defense.*

RECOMMENDATION 56: *The U.S. Department of Justice should direct the training mission of the police forces remaining under the Ministry of the Interior.*

RECOMMENDATION 57: Just as U.S. military training teams are imbedded within Iraqi Army units, the current practice of imbedding U.S. police trainers should be expanded and the numbers of civilian training officers increased so that teams can cover all levels of the Iraqi Police Service, including local police stations. These trainers should be obtained from among experienced civilian police executives and supervisors from around the world. These officers would replace the military police personnel currently assigned to training teams.

The Federal Bureau of Investigation has provided personnel to train the Criminal Investigation Division in the Ministry of the Interior, which handles major crimes. The FBI has also fielded a large team within Iraq for counterterrorism activities.

Building on this experience, the training programs should be expanded and should include the development of forensic investigation training and facilities that could apply scientific and technical investigative methods to counterterrorism as well as to ordinary criminal activity.

RECOMMENDATION 58: The FBI should expand its investigative and forensic training and facilities within Iraq, to include coverage of terrorism as well as criminal activity.

One of the major deficiencies of the Iraqi Police Service is its lack of equipment, particularly in the area of communications and motor transport.

RECOMMENDATION 59: The Iraqi government should provide funds to expand and upgrade communications equipment and motor vehicles for the Iraqi Police Service.

The Department of Justice is also better suited than the Department of Defense to carry out the mission of reforming Iraq's Ministry of the Interior and Iraq's judicial system. Iraq needs more than training for cops on the beat: it needs courts, trained prosecutors and investigators, and the ability to protect Iraqi judicial officials.

RECOMMENDATION 60: The U.S. Department of Justice should lead the work of organizational transformation in the Ministry of the Interior. This approach must involve Iraqi officials, starting at senior levels and moving down, to create a strategic plan and work out standard administrative procedures, codes of conduct, and operational measures that Iraqis will accept and use. These plans must be drawn up in partnership.

RECOMMENDATION 61: Programs led by the U.S. Department of Justice to establish courts; to train judges, prosecutors, and investigators; and to create institutions and practices to fight corruption must be strongly supported and funded. New and refurbished courthouses with improved physical security, secure housing for judges and judicial staff, witness protection facilities, and a new Iraqi Marshals Service are essential parts of a secure and functioning system of justice.

5. The Oil Sector

Since the success of the oil sector is critical to the success of the Iraqi economy, the United States must do what it can to help Iraq maximize its capability.

Iraq, a country with promising oil potential, could restore oil production from existing fields to 3.0 to 3.5 million barrels a day over a three- to five-year period, depending on evolving conditions in key reservoirs. Even if Iraq were at peace tomorrow, oil production would decline unless current problems in the oil sector were addressed.

Short Term

RECOMMENDATION 62:

- *As soon as possible, the U.S. government should provide technical assistance to the Iraqi government to prepare a draft oil law that defines the rights of regional and local governments and creates a fiscal and legal framework for investment. Legal clarity is essential to attract investment.*

- *The U.S. government should encourage the Iraqi government to accelerate contracting for the comprehensive well work-overs in the southern fields needed to increase production, but the United States should no longer fund such infrastructure projects.*

- *The U.S. military should work with the Iraqi military and with private security forces to protect oil infrastructure and contractors. Protective measures could include a program to improve pipeline security by paying local tribes solely on the basis of throughput (rather than fixed amounts).*

- *Metering should be implemented at both ends of the supply line. This step would immediately improve accountability in the oil sector.*

- *In conjunction with the International Monetary Fund, the U.S. government should press Iraq to continue reducing subsidies in the energy sector, instead of providing grant assistance. Until Iraqis pay market prices for oil products, drastic fuel shortages will remain.*

Long Term

Expanding oil production in Iraq over the long term will require creating corporate structures, establishing management systems, and installing competent managers to plan and oversee an ambitious list of major oil-field investment projects.

To improve oil-sector performance, the Study Group puts forward the following recommendations.

RECOMMENDATION 63:

- *The United States should encourage investment in Iraq's oil sector by the international community and by international energy companies.*

- *The United States should assist Iraqi leaders to reorganize the national oil industry as a commercial enterprise, in order to enhance efficiency, transparency, and accountability.*

- *To combat corruption, the U.S. government should urge the Iraqi government to post all oil contracts, volumes, and prices on the Web so that Iraqis and outside observers can track exports and export revenues.*

- *The United States should support the World Bank's efforts to ensure that best practices are used in contracting. This support involves providing Iraqi officials with contracting templates and training them in contracting, auditing, and reviewing audits.*

- *The United States should provide technical assistance to the Ministry of Oil for enhancing maintenance, improving the payments process, managing cash flows, contracting and auditing, and updating professional training programs for management and technical personnel.*

6. U.S. Economic and Reconstruction Assistance

Building the capacity of the Iraqi government should be at the heart of U.S. reconstruction efforts, and capacity building demands additional U.S. resources.

Progress in providing essential government services is necessary to sustain any progress on the political or security front. The period of large U.S.-funded reconstruction projects is over, yet the Iraqi government is still in great need of technical assistance and advice to build the capacity of its institutions. The Iraqi government needs help with all aspects of its operations, including improved procedures, greater delegation of authority, and better internal controls. The strong emphasis on building capable central ministries must be accompanied by efforts to develop functioning, effective provincial government institutions with local citizen participation.

Job creation is also essential. There is no substitute for private-sector job generation, but the Commander's Emergency Response Program is a necessary transitional mechanism until security and the economic climate improve. It provides immediate economic assistance for trash pickup, water, sewers, and electricity in conjunction with clear, hold, and build operations, and it should be funded generously. A total of $753 million was appropriated for this program in FY 2006.

RECOMMENDATION 64: U.S. economic assistance should be increased to a level of $5 billion per year rather than being permitted to decline. The President needs to ask for the necessary resources and must work hard to win the support of Congress. Capacity building and job creation, including reliance on the Commander's Emergency Response Program, should be U.S. priorities. Economic assistance should be provided on a nonsectarian basis.

The New Diplomatic Offensive can help draw in more international partners to assist with the reconstruction mission. The United Nations, the World Bank, the European Union, the Organization for Economic Cooperation and Development, and some Arab League members need to become hands-on participants in Iraq's reconstruction.

RECOMMENDATION 65: An essential part of reconstruction efforts in Iraq should be greater involvement by and with international partners, who should do more than just contribute money. They should also actively participate in the design and construction of projects.

The number of refugees and internally displaced persons within Iraq is increasing dramatically. If this situation is not addressed, Iraq and the region could be further destabilized, and the humanitarian suffering could be severe. Funding for international relief efforts is insufficient, and should be increased.

RECOMMENDATION 66: The United States should take the lead in funding assistance requests from the United Nations High Commissioner for Refugees, and other humanitarian agencies.

Coordination of Economic and Reconstruction Assistance

A lack of coordination by senior management in Washington still hampers U.S. contributions to Iraq's reconstruction.

Focus, priority setting, and skillful implementation are in short supply. No single official is assigned responsibility or held accountable for the overall reconstruction effort. Representatives of key foreign partners involved in reconstruction have also spoken to us directly and specifically about the need for a point of contact that can coordinate their efforts with the U.S. government.

A failure to improve coordination will result in agencies continuing to follow conflicting strategies, wasting taxpayer dollars on duplicative and uncoordinated efforts. This waste will further undermine public confidence in U.S. policy in Iraq.

A Senior Advisor for Economic Reconstruction in Iraq is required. He or she should report to the President, be given a staff and funding, and chair a National Security Council interagency group consisting of senior principals at the undersecretary level from all relevant U.S. government departments and agencies. The Senior Advisor's responsibility must be to bring unity of effort to the policy, budget, and implementation of economic reconstruction programs in Iraq. The Senior Advisor must act as the principal point of contact with U.S. partners in the overall reconstruction effort.

He or she must have close and constant interaction with senior U.S. officials and military commanders in Iraq, especially the Director of the Iraq Reconstruction and Management Office, so that the realities on the ground are brought directly and fully into the policy-making process. In order to maximize the effectiveness of assistance, all involved must be on the same page at all times.

RECOMMENDATION 67: The President should create a Senior Advisor for Economic Reconstruction in Iraq.

Improving the Effectiveness of
Assistance Programs

Congress should work with the administration to improve its ability to implement assistance programs in Iraq quickly, flexibly, and effectively.

As opportunities arise, the Chief of Mission in Iraq should have the authority to fund quick-disbursing projects to promote national reconciliation, as well as to rescind funding from programs and projects in which the government of Iraq is not demonstrating effective partnership. These are important tools to improve performance and accountability—as is the work of the Special Inspector General for Iraq Reconstruction.

RECOMMENDATION 68: The Chief of Mission in Iraq should have the authority to spend significant funds through a program structured along the lines of the Commander's Emergency Response Program, and should have the authority to rescind funding from programs and projects in which the government of Iraq is not demonstrating effective partnership.

RECOMMENDATION 69: The authority of the Special Inspector General for Iraq Reconstruction should be renewed for the duration of assistance programs in Iraq.

U.S. security assistance programs in Iraq are slowed considerably by the differing requirements of State and Defense Department programs and of their respective congressional oversight committees. Since Iraqi forces must be trained and equipped, streamlining the provision of training and equipment to Iraq is critical. Security assistance should be delivered promptly, within weeks of a decision to provide it.

RECOMMENDATION 70: A more flexible security assistance program for Iraq, breaking down the barriers to effective interagency cooperation, should be authorized and implemented.

The United States also needs to break down barriers that discourage U.S. partnerships with international donors and Iraqi participants to promote reconstruction. The ability of the United States to form such partnerships will encourage greater international participation in Iraq.

RECOMMENDATION 71: Authority to merge U.S. funds with those from international donors and Iraqi participants on behalf of assistance projects should be provided.

7. Budget Preparation, Presentation, and Review

The public interest is not well served by the government's preparation, presentation, and review of the budget for the war in Iraq.

First, most of the costs of the war show up not in the normal budget request but in requests for emergency supplemental appropriations. This means that funding requests are drawn up outside the normal budget process, are not offset by budgetary reductions elsewhere, and move quickly to the White House with minimal scrutiny. Bypassing the normal review erodes budget discipline and accountability.

Second, the executive branch presents budget requests in a confusing manner, making it difficult for both the general public and members of Congress to understand the request or to differentiate it from counterterrorism operations around the world or operations in Afghanistan. Detailed analyses by budget experts are needed to answer what should be a simple question: "How much money is the President requesting for the war in Iraq?"

Finally, circumvention of the budget process by the executive branch erodes oversight and review by Congress. The authorizing committees (including the House and Senate Armed Services committees) spend the better part of a year reviewing the President's annual budget request. When the President submits an emergency supplemental request, the authorizing committees are bypassed. The request goes directly to the appropriations committees, and they are pressured by the need to act quickly so that troops in the field do not run out of funds. The result is a spending bill that passes Congress with perfunctory review. Even worse, the must-pass appropriations bill becomes loaded with special spending projects that would not survive the normal review process.

RECOMMENDATION 72: Costs for the war in Iraq should be included in the President's annual budget request, starting in FY 2008: the war is in its fourth year, and the normal budget process should not be circumvented. Funding requests for the war in Iraq should be presented clearly to Congress and the American people. Congress must carry out its constitutional responsibility to review budget requests for the war in Iraq carefully and to conduct oversight.

8. U.S. Personnel

The United States can take several steps to ensure that it has personnel with the right skills serving in Iraq.

All of our efforts in Iraq, military and civilian, are handicapped by Americans' lack of language and cultural understanding. Our embassy of 1,000 has 33 Arabic speakers, just six of whom are at the level of fluency. In a conflict that demands effective and efficient communication with Iraqis, we are often at a disadvantage. There are still far too few Arab language–proficient military and civilian officers in Iraq, to the detriment of the U.S. mission.

Civilian agencies also have little experience with complex overseas interventions to restore and maintain order—stability operations—outside of the normal embassy setting. The nature of the mission in Iraq is unfamiliar and dangerous, and the United States has had great difficulty filling civilian assignments in Iraq with sufficient numbers of properly trained personnel at the appropriate rank.

RECOMMENDATION 73: The Secretary of State, the Secretary of Defense, and the Director of National Intelligence should accord the highest possible priority to professional language proficiency and cultural training, in general and specifically for U.S. officers and personnel about to be assigned to Iraq.

RECOMMENDATION 74: *In the short term, if not enough civilians volunteer to fill key positions in Iraq, civilian agencies must fill those positions with directed assignments. Steps should be taken to mitigate familial or financial hardships posed by directed assignments, including tax exclusions similar to those authorized for U.S. military personnel serving in Iraq.*

RECOMMENDATION 75: *For the longer term, the United States government needs to improve how its constituent agencies—Defense, State, Agency for International Development, Treasury, Justice, the intelligence community, and others—respond to a complex stability operation like that represented by this decade's Iraq and Afghanistan wars and the previous decade's operations in the Balkans. They need to train for, and conduct, joint operations across agency boundaries, following the Goldwater-Nichols model that has proved so successful in the U.S. armed services.*

RECOMMENDATION 76: *The State Department should train personnel to carry out civilian tasks associated with a complex stability operation outside of the traditional embassy setting. It should establish a Foreign Service Reserve Corps with personnel and expertise to provide surge capacity for such an operation. Other key civilian agencies, including Treasury, Justice, and Agriculture, need to create similar technical assistance capabilities.*

9. Intelligence

While the United States has been able to acquire good and sometimes superb tactical intelligence on al Qaeda in Iraq, our government still does not understand very well either the insurgency in Iraq or the role of the militias.

A senior commander told us that human intelligence in Iraq has improved from 10 percent to 30 percent. Clearly, U.S. intelligence agencies can and must do better. As mentioned above, an essential part of better intelligence must be improved language and cultural skills. As an intelligence analyst told us, "We rely too much on others to bring information to us, and too often don't understand what is reported back because we do not understand the context of what we are told."

The Defense Department and the intelligence community have not invested sufficient people and resources to understand the political and military threat to American men and women in the armed forces. Congress has appropriated almost $2 billion this year for countermeasures to protect our troops in Iraq against improvised explosive devices, but the administration has not put forward a request to invest comparable resources in trying to understand the people who fabricate, plant, and explode those devices.

We were told that there are fewer than 10 analysts on the job at the Defense Intelligence Agency who have more than two years' experience in analyzing the insurgency. Capable analysts are rotated to new assignments, and on-the-job training begins anew. Agencies must have a better personnel system to keep analytic expertise focused on the insurgency. They are not doing enough to map the insurgency, dissect it, and understand it on a national and provincial level. The analytic community's knowledge of the organization, leadership, financing, and operations of militias, as well as their relationship to government security forces, also falls far short of what policy makers need to know.

In addition, there is significant underreporting of the violence in Iraq. The standard for recording attacks acts as a filter to keep events out of reports and databases. A murder of an Iraqi is not necessarily counted as an attack. If we cannot determine the source of a sectarian attack, that assault does not make it into the database. A roadside bomb or a rocket or mortar attack that doesn't hurt U.S. personnel doesn't count. For example, on one day in July 2006 there were 93 attacks or significant acts of violence reported. Yet a careful review of the reports for that single day brought to light 1,100 acts of violence. Good policy is difficult to make when information is systematically collected in a way that minimizes its discrepancy with policy goals.

RECOMMENDATION 77: *The Director of National Intelligence and the Secretary of Defense should devote significantly greater analytic resources to the task of understanding the threats and sources of violence in Iraq.*

RECOMMENDATION 78: *The Director of National Intelligence and the Secretary of Defense should also institute immediate changes in the collection of data about violence and the sources of violence in Iraq to provide a more accurate picture of events on the ground.*

Recommended Iraqi Actions

The Iraqi government must improve its intelligence capability, initially to work with the United States, and ultimately to take full responsibility for this intelligence function.

To facilitate enhanced Iraqi intelligence capabilities, the CIA should increase its personnel in Iraq to train Iraqi intelligence personnel. The CIA should also develop, with Iraqi officials, a counterterrorism intelligence center for the all-source fusion of information on the various sources of terrorism within Iraq. This center would analyze data concerning the individuals, organizations, networks, and support groups involved in terrorism within Iraq. It would also facilitate intelligence-led police and military actions against them.

RECOMMENDATION 79: The CIA should provide additional personnel in Iraq to develop and train an effective intelligence service and to build a counterterrorism intelligence center that will facilitate intelligence-led counterterrorism efforts.

Appendices

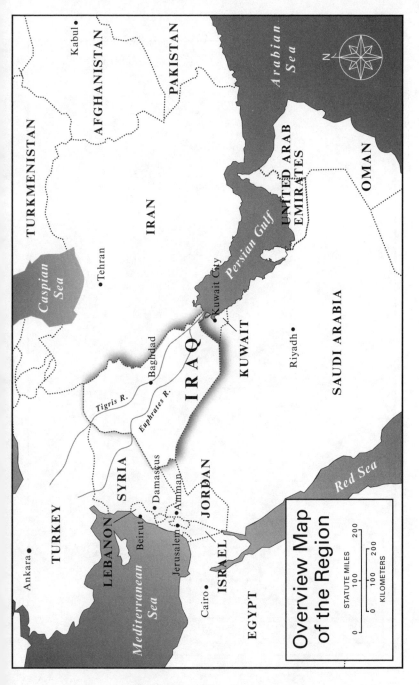

Overview Map
of the Region

STATUTE MILES

0   100   200

0   100   200
KILOMETERS

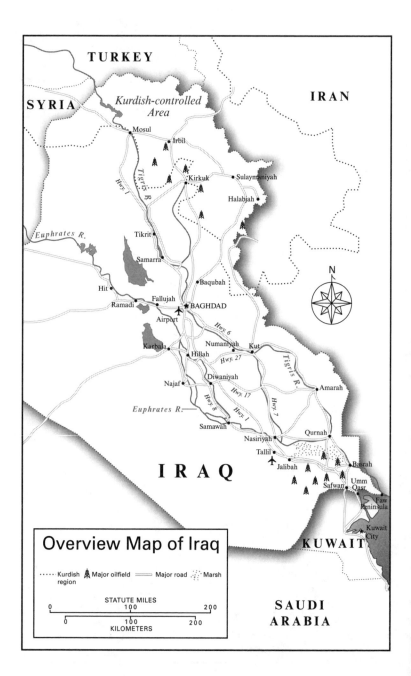

Overview Map of Iraq

····· Kurdish region   ⛏ Major oilfield   ═══ Major road   ⋰ Marsh

STATUTE MILES
0 — 100 — 200

0 — 100 — 200
KILOMETERS

TURKEY

DAHUK

IRAN

ARBIL

SYRIA

NINAWA

AT
TA'MIM

1

SALAH
AD DIN

DIYALA

AL ANBAR

2

IRAQ

3   BABIL

WASIT

4

DHI
QAR

MAYSAN

AN NAJAF

AL MUTHANNA

AL
BASRAH

SAUDI ARABIA

KUWAIT

N

ADMINISTRATIVE DIVISIONS

Iraq has 18 provinces
(muhafazat, singular muhafazah).

⊙ Province capital

1. As Sulaymaniyah
2. Baghdad
3. Karbala
4. Al Qadisiyah

STATUTE MILES
0   100   200

0   100   200
KILOMETERS

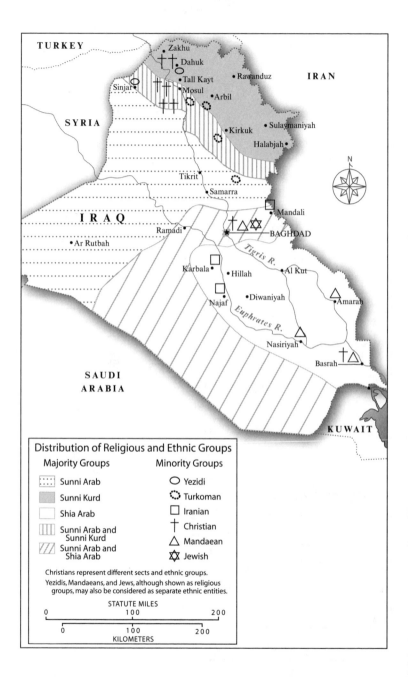

Distribution of Religious and Ethnic Groups

Majority Groups

- Sunni Arab
- Sunni Kurd
- Shia Arab
- Sunni Arab and Sunni Kurd
- Sunni Arab and Shia Arab

Minority Groups

- ◯ Yezidi
- ◌ Turkoman
- ☐ Iranian
- † Christian
- △ Mandaean
- ✡ Jewish

Christians represent different sects and ethnic groups.
Yezidis, Mandaeans, and Jews, although shown as religious groups, may also be considered as separate ethnic entities.

STATUTE MILES
0   100   200

0   100   200
KILOMETERS

Letter from the Sponsoring Organizations

The initiative for a bipartisan, independent, forward-looking "fresh-eyes" assessment of Iraq emerged from conversations U.S. House Appropriations Committee Member Frank Wolf had with us. In late 2005, Congressman Wolf asked the United States Institute of Peace, a bipartisan federal entity, to facilitate the assessment, in collaboration with the James A. Baker, III Institute for Public Policy at Rice University, the Center for the Study of the Presidency, and the Center for Strategic and International Studies.

Interested members of Congress, in consultation with the sponsoring organizations and the administration, agreed that former Republican U.S. Secretary of State James A. Baker, III and former Democratic Congressman Lee H. Hamilton had the breadth of knowledge of foreign affairs required to co-chair this bipartisan effort. The co-chairs subsequently selected the other members of the bipartisan Iraq Study Group, all senior individuals with distinguished records of public service. Democrats included former Secretary of Defense William J. Perry, former Governor and U.S. Senator Charles S. Robb, former Congressman and White House chief of staff Leon E. Panetta, and Vernon E. Jordan, Jr., advisor to President Bill Clinton. Republicans included former Associate Justice to the U.S. Supreme Court Sandra Day O'Connor, former U.S. Senator Alan K. Simpson, former Attorney General Edwin Meese III, and former Secretary of State Lawrence S. Eagleburger. Former CIA Director Robert Gates was an active member for a period of months until his nomination as Secretary of Defense.

The Iraq Study Group was launched on March 15, 2006, in a Capitol Hill meeting hosted by U.S. Senator John Warner and attended by congressional leaders from both sides of the aisle.

To support the Study Group, the sponsoring organizations created four expert working groups consisting of 44 leading foreign policy analysts and specialists on Iraq. The working groups, led by staff of the United States Institute of Peace, focused on the Strategic Environment, Military and Security Issues, Political Development, and the Economy and Reconstruction. Every effort was made to ensure the participation of experts across a wide span of the political spectrum. Additionally, a panel of retired military officers was consulted.

We are grateful to all those who have assisted the Study Group, especially the supporting experts and staff. Our thanks go to Daniel P. Serwer of the Institute of Peace, who served as executive director; Christopher Kojm, advisor to the Study Group; John Williams, Policy Assistant to Mr. Baker; and Ben Rhodes, Special Assistant to Mr. Hamilton.

Richard H. Solomon, *President*
United States Institute of Peace

Edward P. Djerejian, *Founding Director*
James A. Baker III Institute for Public Policy,
Rice University

Letter from the Sponsoring Organizations

David M. Abshire, *President*
Center for the Study of the Presidency

John J. Hamre, *President*
Center for Strategic and International Studies

Iraq Study Group Plenary Sessions

March 15, 2006
April 11–12, 2006
May 18–19, 2005
June 13–14, 2006
August 2–3, 2006
August 30–September 4, 2006 (Trip to Baghdad)
September 18–19, 2006
November 13–14, 2006
November 27–29, 2006

Iraq Study Group Consultations

(° denotes a meeting that took place in Iraq)

Iraqi Officials and Representatives

° Jalal Talabani—*President*
° Tariq al-Hashimi—*Vice President*
° Adil Abd al-Mahdi—*Vice President*
° Nouri Kamal al-Maliki—*Prime Minister*
° Salaam al-Zawbai—*Deputy Prime Minister*
° Barham Salih—*Deputy Prime Minister*
° Mahmoud al-Mashhadani—*Speaker of the Parliament*
° Mowaffak al-Rubaie—*National Security Advisor*
° Jawad Kadem al-Bolani—*Minister of Interior*
° Abdul Qader Al-Obeidi—*Minister of Defense*
° Hoshyar Zebari—*Minister of Foreign Affairs*
° Bayan Jabr—*Minister of Finance*
° Hussein al-Shahristani—*Minster of Oil*
° Karim Waheed—*Minister of Electricity*
° Akram al-Hakim—*Minister of State for National
    Reconciliation Affairs*
° Mithal al-Alusi—*Member, High Commission on National
    Reconciliation*

° Ayad Jamal al-Din—*Member, High Commission on National Reconciliation*

° Ali Khalifa al-Duleimi—*Member, High Commission on National Reconciliation*

° Sami al-Ma'ajoon—*Member, High Commission on National Reconciliation*

° Muhammad Ahmed Mahmoud—*Member, Commission on National Reconciliation*

° Wijdan Mikhael—*Member, High Commission on National Reconciliation*

Lt. General Nasir Abadi—*Deputy Chief of Staff of the Iraqi Joint Forces*

° Adnan al-Dulaimi—*Head of the Tawafuq list*

Ali Allawi—*Former Minister of Finance*

° Sheik Najeh al-Fetlawi—*representative of Moqtada al-Sadr*

° Abd al-Aziz al-Hakim—*Shia Coalition Leader*

° Sheik Maher al-Hamraa—*Ayat Allah Said Sussein Al Sadar*

° Hajim al-Hassani—*Member of the Parliament on the Iraqiya list*

° Hunain Mahmood Ahmed Al-Kaddo—*President of the Iraqi Minorities Council*

° Abid al-Gufhoor Abid al-Razaq al-Kaisi—*Dean of the Islamic University of the Imam Al-Atham*

° Ali Neema Mohammed Aifan al-Mahawili—*Rafiday Al-Iraq Al-Jaded Foundation*

° Saleh al-Mutlaq—*Leader of the Iraqi Front for National Dialogue*

° Ayyad al-Sammara'l—*Member of the Parliament*

° Yonadim Kenna—*Member of the Parliament and Secretary General of Assyrian Movement*

° Shahla Wali Mohammed—*Iraqi Counterpart International*

* Hamid Majid Musa—*Secretary of the Iraqi Communist Party*
* Raid Khyutab Muhemeed—*Humanitarian, Cultural, and Social Foundation*

Sinan Shabibi—*Governor of the Central Bank of Iraq*

Samir Shakir M. Sumaidaie—*Ambassador of Iraq to the United States*

Current U.S. Administration Officials

Senior Administration Officials

George W. Bush—*President*
Richard B. Cheney—*Vice President*
Condoleezza Rice—*Secretary of State*
Donald H. Rumsfeld—*Secretary of Defense*
Stephen J. Hadley—*National Security Advisor*
Joshua B. Bolten—*White House Chief of Staff*

Department of Defense/Military

CIVILIAN:
Gordon England—*Deputy Secretary of Defense*
Stephen Cambone—*Under Secretary of Defense for Intelligence*
Eric Edelman—*Under Secretary of Defense for Policy*

MILITARY:
General Peter Pace—*Chairman of the Joint Chiefs of Staff*
Admiral Edmund Giambastiani—*Vice-Chairman of the Joint Chiefs of Staff*
General John Abizaid—*Commander, United States Central Command*

Iraq Study Group Consultations

° General George W. Casey, Jr.—*Commanding General, Multi-National Forces–Iraq*

Lt. General James T. Conway—*Director of Operations, J-3, on the Joint Staff*

° Lt. General Peter Chiarelli—*Commander, Multi-National Forces–Iraq*

Lt. General David H. Petraeus—*Commanding General, U.S. Army Combined Arms Center and Fort Leavenworth*

° Lt. General Martin Dempsey—*Commander Multi-National Security Transition Command–Iraq*

° Maj. General Joseph Peterson—*Coalition Police Assistance Training Team*

° Maj. General Richard Zilmer—Commander, 1st Marine Expeditionary Force

Colonel Derek Harvey—*Senior Intelligence Officer for Iraq, Defense Intelligence Agency*

Lt. Colonel Richard Bowyer—*National War College (recently served in Iraq)*

Lt. Colonel Justin Gubler—*National War College (recently served in Iraq)*

Lt. Colonel David Haight—*National War College (recently served in Iraq)*

Lt. Colonel Russell Smith—*National War College (recently served in Iraq)*

Department of State/Civilian Embassy Personnel

R. Nicholas Burns—*Under Secretary of State for Political Affairs*

Philip Zelikow—*Counselor to the Department of State*

C. David Welch—*Assistant Secretary of State for Near Eastern Affairs*

James Jeffrey—*Senior Advisor to Secretary Rice and Coordinator for Iraq Policy*

David Satterfield—*Senior Advisor to Secretary Rice and Coordinator for Iraq Policy*

Zalmay Khalilzad—*U.S. Ambassador to Iraq*

* Dan Speckhard—*Charge D'Affaires, U.S. Embassy in Iraq*

* Joseph Saloom—*Director, Iraq Reconstruction and Management Office*

* Hilda Arellano—*U.S. Agency for International Development Director in Iraq*

* Terrance Kelly—*Director, Office of Strategic Plans and Assessments*

* Randall Bennett—*Regional Security Officer of the U.S. Embassy, Baghdad, Iraq*

Intelligence Community

John D. Negroponte—*Director of National Intelligence*

General Michael V. Hayden—*Director, Central Intelligence Agency*

Thomas Fingar—*Deputy Director of National Intelligence for Analysis and Chairman of the National Intelligence Council*

John Sherman—*Deputy National Intelligence Officer for Military Issues*

Steve Ward—*Deputy National Intelligence Officer for the Middle East*

Jeff Wickham—*Iraq Analyst, Central Intelligence Agency*

Other Senior Officials

David Walker—*Comptroller General of the United States*

* Stuart Bowen—*Special Inspector General for Iraqi Reconstruction*

Iraq Study Group Consultations

Members of Congress

United States Senate

Senator William Frist (R-TN)—*Majority Leader*

Senators Harry Reid (D-NV)—*Minority Leader*

Senator Mitch McConnell (R-KY)—*Majority Whip*

Senator Richard Durbin (D-IL)—*Minority Whip*

Senator Richard Lugar (R-IN)—*Chair, Foreign Relations
    Committee*

Senators John Warner (R-VA)—*Chair, Armed Services
    Committee*

Senator Joseph Biden (D-DE)—*Ranking Member, Foreign
    Relations Committee*

Senator Carl Levin (D-MI)—*Ranking Member, Armed
    Services Committee*

Senator Jeff Bingaman (D-NM)—*Ranking Member, Energy
    and Resources Committee*

Senator Kit Bond (R-MO)—*Member, Intelligence
    Committee*

Senator James Inhofe (R-OK)—*Member, Armed Services
    Committee*

Senator John Kerry (D-MA)—*Member, Foreign Relations
    Committee*

Senator Joseph Lieberman (D-CT)—*Member, Armed
    Services Committee*

Senator John McCain (R-AZ)—*Member, Armed Services
    Committee*

Senator Jack Reed (D-RI)—*Member, Armed Services
    Committee*

United States House of Representatives

Representative Nancy Pelosi (D-CA)—*Minority Leader*

Representative Tom Davis (R-VA)—*Chair, Government Reform Committee*

Representative Jane Harman (D-CA)—*Ranking Member, Intelligence Committee*

Representative Ike Skelton (D-MO)—*Ranking Member, Armed Services Committee*

Representative John Murtha (D-PA)—*Ranking Member, Appropriations Subcommittee on Defense*

Representative Jim Cooper (D-TN)—*Member, Armed Services Committee*

Representative Michael McCaul (R-TX)—*Member, International Relations Committee*

Representative Alan Mollohan (D-WV)—*Member, Appropriations Committee*

Representative Christopher Shays (R-CT)—*Member, Government Reform Committee*

Representative Frank Wolf (R-VA)—*Member, Appropriations Committee*

Foreign Officials

Sheikh Salem al-Abdullah al-Sabah—*Ambassador of Kuwait to the United States*

David Abramovich—*Director General of the Israeli Ministry of Foreign Affairs*

Michael Ambuhl—*Secretary of State of Switzerland*

Kofi Annan—*Secretary-General of the United Nations*

* Dominic Asquith—*British Ambassador to Iraq*

Tony Blair—*Prime Minister of the United Kingdom*

Prince Turki al-Faisal—*Ambassador of Saudi Arabia to the United States*
Nabil Fahmy—*Ambassador of Egypt to the United States*
Karim Kawar—*Ambassador of Jordan to the United States*
Nasser bin Hamad al-Khalifa—*Ambassador of Qatar to the United States*
* Mukhtar Lamani—*Arab League envoy to Iraq*
Sir David Manning—*British Ambassador to the United States*
Imad Moustapha—*Ambassador of Syria to the United States*
Walid Muallem—*Foreign Minister of Syria*
Romano Prodi—*Prime Minister of Italy*
* Ashraf Qazi—*Special Representative of the UN Secretary-General for Iraq*
Anders Fogh Rasmussen—*Prime Minister of Denmark*
Nabi Sensoy—*Ambassador of Turkey to the United States*
Ephraim Sneh—*Deputy Minister of Defense of the State of Israel*
Javad Zarif—*Iranian Ambassador to the United Nations*
Sheikh Abdullah bin Zayad—*Minister of Foreign Affairs of the United Arab Emirates*

Former Officials and Experts

William J. Clinton—*former President of the United States*
Walter Mondale—*former Vice President of the United States*
Madeleine K. Albright—*former United States Secretary of State*
Warren Christopher—*former United States Secretary of State*
Henry Kissinger—*former United States Secretary of State*
Colin Powell—*former United States Secretary of State*
George P. Schultz—*former United States Secretary of State*

Samuel R. Berger—*former United States National Security Advisor*

Zbigniew Brzezinski—*former United States National Security Advisor*

Anthony Lake—*former United States National Security Advisor*

General Brent Scowcroft—*former United States National Security Advisor*

General Eric Shinseki—*former Chief of Staff of the United States Army*

General Anthony Zinni—*former Commander, United States Central Command*

General John Keane—*former Vice Chief of Staff of the United States Army*

Admiral Jim Ellis—*former Commander of United States Strategic Command*

General Joe Ralston—*former Supreme Allied Commander of NATO*

Lt. General Roger C. Schultz—*former Director of the United States Army National Guard*

Douglas Feith—*former United States Under Secretary of Defense for Policy*

Mark Danner—*The New York Review of Books*

Larry Diamond—*Senior Fellow at the Hoover Institution, Stanford University*

Thomas Friedman—*New York Times*

Leslie Gelb—*President Emeritus, Council on Foreign Relations*

Richard Hill—*Director, Office of Strategic Initiatives and Analysis, CHF International*

Richard C. Holbrooke—*former Ambassador of the United States to the United Nations*

Martin S. Indyk—*Director, Saban Center for Middle East Policy, The Brookings Institution*

Ronald Johnson—*Executive Vice President for International Development, RTI International*

Frederick Kagan—*The American Enterprise Institute*

Arthur Keys, Jr.—*President and CEO, International Relief and Development*

William Kristol—*The Weekly Standard*

* Guy Laboa—*Kellogg, Brown & Root*

Nancy Lindborg—*President, Mercy Corps*

Michael O'Hanlon—*Senior Fellow, Foreign Policy Studies, The Brookings Institution*

George Packer—*The New Yorker*

Carlos Pascual—*Vice President and Director, Foreign Policy Studies, The Brookings Institution*

Robert Perito—*Senior Program Officer, United States Institute of Peace*

* Col. Jack Petri, USA (Ret.)—*advisor to the Iraqi Ministry of Interior*

Kenneth Pollack—*Director of Research, Saban Center for Middle East Policy, The Brookings Institution*

Thomas Ricks—*The Washington Post*

Zainab Salbi—*Founder and CEO, Women for Women International*

Matt Sherman—*former Deputy Senior Advisor and Director of Policy, Iraqi Ministry of Interior*

Strobe Talbott—*President, The Brookings Institution*

Rabih Torbay—*Vice President for International Operations, International Medical Corps*

George Will—*The Washington Post*

Expert Working Groups and Military Senior Advisor Panel

Economy and Reconstruction

Gary Matthews, USIP Secretariat
Director, Task Force on the United Nations and Special Projects, United States Institute of Peace

Raad Alkadiri
Director, Country Strategies Group, PFC Energy

Frederick D. Barton
Senior Adviser and Co-Director, International Security Program, Center for Strategic & International Studies

Jay Collins
Chief Executive Officer, Public Sector Group, Citigroup, Inc.

Jock P. Covey
Senior Vice President, External Affairs, Corporate Security and Sustainability Services, Bechtel Corporation

Expert Working Groups

Keith Crane
Senior Economist, RAND Corporation

Amy Myers Jaffe
Associate Director for Energy Studies, James A. Baker III Institute for Public Policy, Rice University

K. Riva Levinson
Managing Director, BKSH & Associates

David A. Lipton
Managing Director and Head of Global Country Risk Management, Citigroup, Inc

Michael E. O'Hanlon
Senior Fellow, Foreign Policy Studies, The Brookings Institution

James A. Placke
Senior Associate, Cambridge Energy Research Associates

James A. Schear
Director of Research, Institute for National Strategic Studies, National Defense University

Military and Security

Paul Hughes, USIP Secretariat
Senior Program Officer, Center for Post-Conflict Peace and Stability Operations, United States Institute of Peace

Expert Working Groups

Hans A. Binnendijk
Director & Theodore Roosevelt Chair, Center for Technology
& National Security Policy, National Defense University

James Carafano
Senior Research Fellow, Defense and Homeland Security,
Douglas and Sarah Allison Center for Foreign Policy Studies,
The Heritage Foundation

Michael Eisenstadt
Director, Military & Security Program, The Washington
Institute for Near East Policy

Michèle A. Flournoy
Senior Advisor, International Security Program, Center for
Strategic & International Studies

Bruce Hoffman
Professor, Security Studies Program, Edmund A. Walsh School
of Foreign Service, Georgetown University

Clifford May
President, Foundation for the Defense of Democracies

Robert M. Perito
Senior Program Officer, Center for Post-Conflict Peace and
Stability Operations, United States Institute of Peace

Kalev I. Sepp
Assistant Professor, Department of Defense Analysis, Center
on Terrorism and Irregular Warfare, Naval Postgraduate School

John F. Sigler
Adjunct Distinguished Professor, Near East South Asia Center for Strategic Studies, National Defense University

W. Andrew Terrill
Research Professor, National Security Affairs, Strategic Studies Institute

Jeffrey A. White
Berrie Defense Fellow, Washington Institute for Near East Policy

Political Development

Daniel P. Serwer, USIP Secretariat
Vice President, Center for Post-Conflict Peace and Stability Operations, United States Institute of Peace

Raymond H. Close
Freelance Analyst and Commentator on Middle East Politics

Larry Diamond
Senior Fellow, The Hoover Institution, Stanford University, and Co-Editor, Journal of Democracy

Andrew P. N. Erdmann
Former Director for Iran, Iraq and Strategic Planning, National Security Council

Reuel Marc Gerecht
Resident Fellow, American Enterprise Institute

Expert Working Groups

David L. Mack
Vice President, The Middle East Institute

Phebe A. Marr
Senior Fellow, United States Institute of Peace

Hassan Mneimneh
Director, Documentation Program, The Iraq Memory Foundation

Augustus Richard Norton
Professor of International Relations and Anthropology, Department of International Relations, Boston University

Marina S. Ottaway
Senior Associate, Democracy and Rule of Law Project, Carnegie Endowment for International Peace

Judy Van Rest
Executive Vice President, International Republican Institute

Judith S. Yaphe
Distinguished Research Fellow for the Middle East, Institute for National Strategic Studies, National Defense University

Strategic Environment

Paul Stares, USIP Secretariat
Vice President, Center for Conflict Analysis and Prevention, United States Institute of Peace

Expert Working Groups

Jon B. Alterman
Director, Middle East Program, Center for Strategic &
International Studies

Steven A. Cook
Douglas Dillon Fellow, Council on Foreign Relations

James F. Dobbins
Director, International Security and Defense Policy Center,
RAND Corporation

Hillel Fradkin
Director, Center for Islam, Democracy and the Future of the
Muslim World, Hudson Institute

Chas W. Freeman
Chairman, Projects International and President, Middle East
Policy Council

Geoffrey Kemp
Director, Regional Strategic Programs, The Nixon Center

Daniel C. Kurtzer
S. Daniel Abraham Visiting Professor, Middle East Policy
Studies, Woodrow Wilson School, Princeton University

Ellen Laipson
President and CEO, The Henry L. Stimson Center

William B. Quandt
Edward R. Stettinius, Jr. Professor of Government and Foreign
Affairs, University of Virginia, and Nonresident Senior Fellow,
Saban Center for Middle East Policy, The Brookings Institution

Expert Working Groups

Shibley Telhami
Anwar Sadat Chair for Peace and Development, Department of Government & Politics, University of Maryland, and Nonresident Senior Fellow, Saban Center for Middle East Policy, The Brookings Institution

Wayne White
Adjunct Scholar, Public Policy Center, Middle East Institute

Military Senior Advisor Panel

Admiral James O. Ellis, Jr.
United States Navy, Retired

General John M. Keane
United States Army, Retired

General Edward C. Meyer
United States Army, Retired

General Joseph W. Ralston
United States Air Force, Retired

Lieutenant General Roger C. Schultz, Sr.
United States Army, Retired

The Iraq Study Group

James A. Baker, III—Co-Chair

James A. Baker, III has served in senior government positions under three United States presidents. He served as the nation's 61st Secretary of State from January 1989 through August 1992 under President George H. W. Bush. During his tenure at the State Department, Mr. Baker traveled to 90 foreign countries as the United States confronted the unprecedented challenges and opportunities of the post–Cold War era. Mr. Baker's reflections on those years of revolution, war, and peace—*The Politics of Diplomacy*—was published in 1995.

Mr. Baker served as the 67th Secretary of the Treasury from 1985 to 1988 under President Ronald Reagan. As Treasury Secretary, he was also Chairman of the President's Economic Policy Council. From 1981 to 1985, he served as White House Chief of Staff to President Reagan. Mr. Baker's record of public service began in 1975 as Under Secretary of Commerce to President Gerald Ford. It concluded with his service as White House Chief of Staff and Senior Counselor to President Bush from August 1992 to January 1993.

Long active in American presidential politics, Mr. Baker led presidential campaigns for Presidents Ford, Reagan, and

Bush over the course of five consecutive presidential elections from 1976 to 1992.

A native Houstonian, Mr. Baker graduated from Princeton University in 1952. After two years of active duty as a lieutenant in the United States Marine Corps, he entered the University of Texas School of Law at Austin. He received his J.D. with honors in 1957 and practiced law with the Houston firm of Andrews and Kurth from 1957 to 1975.

Mr. Baker's memoir—*Work Hard, Study . . . and Keep Out of Politics! Adventures and Lessons from an Unexpected Public Life*—was published in October 2006.

Mr. Baker received the Presidential Medal of Freedom in 1991 and has been the recipient of many other awards for distinguished public service, including Princeton University's Woodrow Wilson Award, the American Institute for Public Service's Jefferson Award, Harvard University's John F. Kennedy School of Government Award, the Hans J. Morgenthau Award, the George F. Kennan Award, the Department of the Treasury's Alexander Hamilton Award, the Department of State's Distinguished Service Award, and numerous honorary academic degrees.

Mr. Baker is presently a senior partner in the law firm of Baker Botts. He is Honorary Chairman of the James A. Baker III Institute for Public Policy at Rice University and serves on the board of the Howard Hughes Medical Institute. From 1997 to 2004, Mr. Baker served as the Personal Envoy of United Nations Secretary-General Kofi Annan to seek a political solution to the conflict over Western Sahara. In 2003, Mr. Baker was appointed Special Presidential Envoy for President George W. Bush on the issue of Iraqi debt. In 2005, he was co-chair, with former President Jimmy Carter, of the Commission on Federal Election Reform. Since March 2006, Mr. Baker and former

U.S. Congressman Lee H. Hamilton have served as the co-chairs of the Iraq Study Group, a bipartisan blue-ribbon panel on Iraq.

Mr. Baker was born in Houston, Texas, in 1930. He and his wife, the former Susan Garrett, currently reside in Houston, and have eight children and seventeen grandchildren.

Lee H. Hamilton—Co-Chair

Lee H. Hamilton became Director of the Woodrow Wilson International Center for Scholars in January 1999. Previously, Mr. Hamilton served for thirty-four years as a United States Congressman from Indiana. During his tenure, he served as Chairman and Ranking Member of the House Committee on Foreign Affairs (now the Committee on International Relations) and chaired the Subcommittee on Europe and the Middle East from the early 1970s until 1993. He was Chairman of the Permanent Select Committee on Intelligence and the Select Committee to Investigate Covert Arms Transactions with Iran.

Also a leading figure on economic policy and congressional organization, he served as Chair of the Joint Economic Committee as well as the Joint Committee on the Organization of Congress, and was a member of the House Standards of Official Conduct Committee. In his home state of Indiana, Mr. Hamilton worked hard to improve education, job training, and infrastructure. Currently, Mr. Hamilton serves as Director of the Center on Congress at Indiana University, which seeks to educate citizens on the importance of Congress and on how Congress operates within our government.

Mr. Hamilton remains an important and active voice on matters of international relations and American national security. He served as a Commissioner on the United States Commission on National Security in the 21st Century (better known as the Hart-Rudman Commission), was Co-Chair with former Senator Howard Baker of the Baker-Hamilton Commission to Investigate Certain Security Issues at Los Alamos, and was Vice-Chairman of the National Commission on Terrorist Attacks Upon the United States (the 9/11 Commission), which issued its report in July 2004. He is currently a member of the President's Foreign Intelligence Advisory Board and the President's Homeland Security Advisory Council, as well as the Director of the Federal Bureau of Investigation's Advisory Board.

Born in Daytona Beach, Florida, Mr. Hamilton relocated with his family to Tennessee and then to Evansville, Indiana. Mr. Hamilton is a graduate of DePauw University and the Indiana University School of Law, and studied for a year at Goethe University in Germany. Before his election to Congress, he practiced law in Chicago and in Columbus, Indiana. A former high school and college basketball star, he has been inducted into the Indiana Basketball Hall of Fame.

Mr. Hamilton's distinguished service in government has been honored through numerous awards in public service and human rights as well as honorary degrees. He is the author of *A Creative Tension—The Foreign Policy Roles of the President and Congress* (2002) and *How Congress Works and Why You Should Care* (2004), and the coauthor of *Without Precedent: The Inside Story of the 9/11 Commission* (2006).

Lee and his wife, the former Nancy Ann Nelson, have three children—Tracy Lynn Souza, Deborah Hamilton Kremer, and Douglas Nelson Hamilton—and five grandchildren: Christina, Maria, McLouis and Patricia Souza and Lina Ying Kremer.

Lawrence S. Eagleburger—Member

Lawrence S. Eagleburger was sworn in as the 62nd U.S. Secretary of State by President George H. W. Bush on December 8, 1992, and as Deputy Secretary of State on March 20, 1989.

After his entry into the Foreign Service in 1957, Mr. Eagleburger served in the U.S. Embassy in Tegucigalpa, Honduras, in the State Department Bureau of Intelligence and Research, in the U.S. Embassy in Belgrade, and the U.S. Mission to NATO in Belgium. In 1963, after a severe earthquake in Macedonia, he led the U.S. government effort to provide medical and other assistance. He was then assigned to Washington, D.C., where he served on the Secretariat staff and as special assistant to Dean Acheson, advisor to the President on Franco-NATO issues. In August 1966, he became acting director of the Secretariat staff.

In October 1966, Mr. Eagleburger joined the National Security Council staff. In October 1967, he was assigned as special assistant to Under Secretary of State Nicholas Katzenbach. In November 1968, he was appointed Dr. Henry Kissinger's assistant, and in January 1969, he became executive assistant to Dr. Kissinger at the White House. In September 1969, he was assigned as political advisor and chief of the political section of the U.S. Mission to NATO in Brussels.

Mr. Eagleburger became Deputy Assistant Secretary of Defense in August 1971. Two years later, he became Acting Assistant Secretary of Defense for International Security Affairs. The same year he returned to the White House as Deputy Assistant to the President for National Security Operations. He subsequently followed Dr. Kissinger to the State Department, becoming Executive Assistant to the Secretary of State. In 1975, he was made Deputy Under Secretary of State for Management.

In June 1977, Mr. Eagleburger was appointed Ambassador to Yugoslavia, and in 1981 he was nominated as Assistant Secretary of State for European Affairs. In February 1982, he was appointed Under Secretary of State for Political Affairs.

Mr. Eagleburger has received numerous awards, including an honorary knighthood from Her Majesty, Queen Elizabeth II (1994); the Distinguished Service Award (1992), the Wilbur J. Carr Award (1984), and the Distinguished Honor Award (1984) from the Department of State; the Distinguished Civilian Service Medal from the Department of Defense (1978); and the President's Award for Distinguished Federal Civilian Service (1976).

After retiring from the Department of State in May 1984, Mr. Eagleburger was named president of Kissinger Associates, Inc. Following his resignation as Secretary of State on January 19, 1993, he joined the law firm of Baker, Donelson, Bearman and Caldwell as Senior Foreign Policy Advisor. He joined the boards of Halliburton Company, Phillips Petroleum Company, and Universal Corporation. Mr. Eagleburger currently serves as Chairman of the International Commission on Holocaust Era Insurance Claims.

He received his B.S. degree in 1952 and his M.S. degree in 1957, both from the University of Wisconsin, and served as first lieutenant in the U.S. Army from 1952 to 1954. Mr. Eagleburger is married to the former Marlene Ann Heinemann. He is the father of three sons, Lawrence Scott, Lawrence Andrew, and Lawrence Jason.

Vernon E. Jordan, Jr.—Member

Vernon E. Jordan, Jr., is a Senior Managing Director of Lazard Frères & Co, LLC in New York. He works with a diverse group of clients across a broad range of industries.

Prior to joining Lazard, Mr. Jordan was a Senior Executive Partner with the law firm of Akin Gump Strauss Hauer & Feld, LLP, where he remains Senior Counsel. While there Mr. Jordan practiced general, corporate, legislative, and international law in Washington, D.C.

Before Akin Gump, Mr. Jordan held the following positions: President and Chief Executive Officer of the National Urban League, Inc.; Executive Director of the United Negro College Fund, Inc.; Director of the Voter Education Project of the Southern Regional Council; Attorney-Consultant, U.S. Office of Economic Opportunity; Assistant to the Executive Director of the Southern Regional Council; Georgia Field Director of the National Association for the Advancement of Colored People; and an attorney in private practice in Arkansas and Georgia.

Mr. Jordan's presidential appointments include the President's Advisory Committee for the Points of Light Initiative Foundation, the Secretary of State's Advisory Committee on South Africa, the Advisory Council on Social Security, the Presidential Clemency Board, the American Revolution Bicentennial Commission, the National Advisory Committee on Selective Service, and the Council of the White House Conference "To Fulfill These Rights." In 1992, Mr. Jordan served as the Chairman of the Clinton Presidential Transition Team.

Mr. Jordan's corporate and other directorships include American Express Company; Asbury Automotive Group, Inc.; Howard University (Trustee); J. C. Penney Company, Inc.;

Lazard Ltd.; Xerox Corporation; and the International Advisory Board of Barrick Gold.

Mr. Jordan is a graduate of DePauw University and the Howard University Law School. He holds honorary degrees from more than 60 colleges and universities in America. He is a member of the bars of Arkansas, the District of Columbia, Georgia, and the U.S. Supreme Court. He is a member of the American Bar Association, the National Bar Association, the Council on Foreign Relations, and the Bilderberg Meetings and he is President of the Economic Club of Washington, D.C. Mr. Jordan is the author of *Vernon Can Read! A Memoir* (Public Affairs, 2001).

Edwin Meese III—Member

Edwin Meese III holds the Ronald Reagan Chair in Public Policy at the Heritage Foundation, a Washington, D.C.–based public policy research and education institution. He is also the Chairman of Heritage's Center for Legal and Judicial Studies and a distinguished visiting fellow at the Hoover Institution, Stanford University. In addition, Meese lectures, writes, and consults throughout the United States on a variety of subjects.

Meese is the author of *With Reagan: The Inside Story*, which was published by Regnery Gateway in June 1992; co-editor of *Making America Safer*, published in 1997 by the Heritage Foundation; and coauthor of *Leadership, Ethics and Policing*, published by Prentice Hall in 2004.

Meese served as the 75th Attorney General of the United States from February 1985 to August 1988. As the nation's chief law enforcement officer, he directed the Department of Justice and led international efforts to combat terrorism, drug trafficking, and organized crime. In 1985 he received *Government Executive* magazine's annual award for excellence in management.

From January 1981 to February 1985, Meese held the position of Counsellor to the President, the senior position on the White House staff, where he functioned as the President's chief policy advisor. As Attorney General and as Counsellor, Meese was a member of the President's cabinet and the National Security Council. He served as Chairman of the Domestic Policy Council and of the National Drug Policy Board. Meese headed the President-elect's transition effort following the November 1980 election. During the presidential campaign, he served as chief of staff and senior issues advisor for the Reagan-Bush Committee.

Formerly, Meese served as Governor Reagan's executive assistant and chief of staff in California from 1969 through 1974 and as legal affairs secretary from 1967 through 1968. Before joining Governor Reagan's staff in 1967, Meese served as deputy district attorney in Alameda County, California. From 1977 to 1981, Meese was a professor of law at the University of San Diego, where he also was Director of the Center for Criminal Justice Policy and Management.

In addition to his background as a lawyer, educator, and public official, Meese has been a business executive in the aerospace and transportation industry, serving as vice president for administration of Rohr Industries, Inc., in Chula Vista, California. He left Rohr to return to the practice of law, engaging in corporate and general legal work in San Diego County.

Meese is a graduate of Yale University, Class of 1953, and holds a law degree from the University of California at Berkeley. He is a retired colonel in the United States Army Reserve. He is active in numerous civic and educational organizations. Meese is married, has two grown children, and resides in McLean, Virginia.

Sandra Day O'Connor—Member

Sandra Day O'Connor was nominated by President Reagan as Associate Justice of the United States Supreme Court on July 7, 1981, and took the oath of office on September 25. O'Connor previously served on the Arizona Court of Appeals (1979–81) and as judge of the Maricopa County Superior Court in Phoenix, Arizona (1975–79). She was appointed as Arizona state senator in 1969 and was subsequently elected to two two-year terms from 1969 to 1975. During her tenure, she was Arizona Senate Majority Leader and Chairman of the State, County, and Municipal Affairs Committee, and she served on the Legislative Council, on the Probate Code Commission, and on the Arizona Advisory Council on Intergovernmental Relations.

From 1965 to 1969, O'Connor was assistant attorney general in Arizona. She practiced law at a private firm in Maryvale, Arizona, from 1958 to 1960 and prior to that was civilian attorney for Quartermaster Market Center in Frankfurt, Germany (1954–57), and deputy county attorney in San Mateo County, California (1952–53)

She was previously Chairman of the Arizona Supreme Court Committee to Reorganize Lower Courts (1974–75), Vice Chairman of the Arizona Select Law Enforcement Review Commission (1979–80), and, in Maricopa County, Chairman of the Bar Association Lawyer Referral Service (1960–62), the Juvenile Detention Home Visiting Board (1963–64), and the Superior Court Judges' Training and Education Committee (1977–79) and a member of the Board of Adjustments and Appeals (1963–64).

O'Connor currently serves as Chancellor of the College of William and Mary and on the Board of Trustees of the

Rockefeller Foundation, the Executive Board of the Central European and Eurasian Law Initiative, the Advisory Board of the Smithsonian National Museum of Natural History, and the Advisory Committee of the American Society of International Law, Judicial. She is an honorary member of the Advisory Committee for the Judiciary Leadership Development Council, an honorary chair of America's 400th Anniversary: Jamestown 2007, a co-chair of the National Advisory Council of the Campaign for the Civic Mission of Schools, a member of the Selection Committee of the Oklahoma City National Memorial & Museum, and a member of the Advisory Board of the Stanford Center on Ethics. She also serves on several bodies of the American Bar Association, including the Museum of Law Executive Committee, the Commission on Civic Education and Separation of Powers, and the Advisory Commission of the Standing Committee on the Law Library of Congress.

O'Connor previously served as a member of the Anglo-American Exchange (1980); the State Bar of Arizona Committees on Legal Aid, Public Relations, Lower Court Reorganization, and Continuing Legal Education; the National Defense Advisory Committee on Women in the Services (1974–76); the Arizona State Personnel Commission (1968–69); the Arizona Criminal Code Commission (1974–76); and the Cathedral Chapter of the Washington National Cathedral (1991–99).

O'Connor is a member of the American Bar Association, the State Bar of Arizona, the State Bar of California, the Maricopa County Bar Association, the Arizona Judges' Association, the National Association of Women Judges, and the Arizona Women Lawyers' Association. She holds a B.A. (with Great Distinction) and an LL.B. (Order of the Coif) from Stanford University, where she was also a member of the board of editors of the *Stanford Law Review*.

Leon E. Panetta—Member

Leon E. Panetta currently co-directs the Leon & Sylvia Panetta Institute for Public Policy, a nonpartisan study center for the advancement of public policy based at California State University, Monterey Bay. He serves as distinguished scholar to the chancellor of the California State University system, teaches a Master's in Public Policy course at the Panetta Institute, is a presidential professor at Santa Clara University, and created the Leon Panetta Lecture Series.

Panetta first went to Washington in 1966, when he served as a legislative assistant to U.S. Senator Thomas H. Kuchel of California. In 1969, he became Special Assistant to the Secretary of Health, Education and Welfare and then Director of the U.S. Office for Civil Rights. His book *Bring Us Together* (published in 1971) is an account of that experience. In 1970, he went to New York City, where he served as Executive Assistant to Mayor John Lindsay. Then, in 1971, Panetta returned to California, where he practiced law in the Monterey firm of Panetta, Thompson & Panetta until he was elected to Congress in 1976.

Panetta was a U.S. Representative from California's 16th (now 17th) district from 1977 to 1993. He authored the Hunger Prevention Act of 1988, the Fair Employment Practices Resolution, legislation that established Medicare and Medicaid reimbursement for hospice care for the terminally ill, and other legislation on a variety of education, health, agriculture, and defense issues.

From 1989 to 1993, Panetta was Chairman of the House Committee on the Budget. He also served on that committee from 1979 to 1985. He chaired the House Agriculture Committee's Subcommittee on Domestic Marketing, Consumer

Relations and Nutrition; the House Administration Committee's Subcommittee on Personnel and Police; and the Select Committee on Hunger's Task Force on Domestic Hunger. He also served as Vice Chairman of the Caucus of Vietnam Era Veterans in Congress and as a member of the President's Commission on Foreign Language and International Studies.

Panetta left Congress in 1993 to become Director of the Office of Management and Budget for the incoming Clinton administration. Panetta was appointed Chief of Staff to the President of the United States on July 17, 1994, and served in that position until January 20, 1997.

In addition, Panetta served a six-year term on the Board of Directors of the New York Stock Exchange beginning in 1997. He currently serves on many public policy and organizational boards, including as Chair of the Pew Oceans Commission and Co-Chair of the California Council on Base Support and Retention.

Panetta has received many awards and honors, including the Smithsonian Paul Peck Award for Service to the Presidency, the John H. Chafee Coastal Stewardship Award, the Julius A. Stratton Award for Coastal Leadership, and the Distinguished Public Service Medal from the Center for the Study of the Presidency.

He earned a B.A. magna cum laude from Santa Clara University in 1960, and in 1963 received his J.D. from Santa Clara University Law School, where he was an editor of the *Santa Clara Law Review*. He served as a first lieutenant in the Army from 1964 to 1966 and received the Army Commendation Medal. Panetta is married to the former Sylvia Marie Varni. They have three grown sons and five grandchildren.

William J. Perry—Member

William Perry is the Michael and Barbara Berberian Professor at Stanford University, with a joint appointment at the Freeman Spogli Institute for International Studies and the School of Engineering. He is a senior fellow at FSI and serves as co-director of the Preventive Defense Project, a research collaboration of Stanford and Harvard universities.

Perry was the 19th Secretary of Defense of the United States, serving from February 1994 to January 1997. He previously served as Deputy Secretary of Defense (1993–94) and as Under Secretary of Defense for Research and Engineering (1977–81). He is on the board of directors of several emerging high-tech companies and is Chairman of Global Technology Partners.

His previous business experience includes serving as a laboratory director for General Telephone and Electronics (1954–64) and as founder and president of ESL Inc. (1964–77), executive vice president of Hambrecht & Quist Inc. (1981–85), and founder and chairman of Technology Strategies & Alliances (1985–93). He is a member of the National Academy of Engineering and a fellow of the American Academy of Arts and Sciences.

From 1946 to 1947, Perry was an enlisted man in the Army Corps of Engineers, and served in the Army of Occupation in Japan. He joined the Reserve Officer Training Corps in 1948 and was a second lieutenant in the Army Reserves from 1950 to 1955. He has received a number of awards, including the Presidential Medal of Freedom (1997), the Department of Defense Distinguished Service Medal (1980 and 1981), and Outstanding Civilian Service Medals from the Army (1962 and

1997), the Air Force (1997), the Navy (1997), the Defense Intelligence Agency (1977 and 1997), NASA (1981), and the Coast Guard (1997). He received the American Electronic Association's Medal of Achievement (1980), the Eisenhower Award (1996), the Marshall Award (1997), the Forrestal Medal (1994), and the Henry Stimson Medal (1994). The National Academy of Engineering selected him for the Arthur Bueche Medal in 1996. He has received awards from the enlisted personnel of the Army, Navy, and the Air Force.

He has received decorations from the governments of Albania, Bahrain, France, Germany, Hungary, Japan, Korea, Poland, Slovenia, Ukraine, and the United Kingdom. He received a B.S. and M.S. from Stanford University and a Ph.D. from Penn State, all in mathematics.

Charles S. Robb—Member

Charles S. Robb joined the faculty of George Mason University as a Distinguished Professor of Law and Public Policy in 2001. Previously he served as Lieutenant Governor of Virginia, from 1978 to 1982; as Virginia's 64th Governor, from 1982 to 1986; and as a United States Senator, from 1989 to 2001.

While in the Senate he became the only member ever to serve simultaneously on all three national security committees (Intelligence, Armed Services, and Foreign Relations). He also served on the Finance, Commerce, and Budget committees.

Before becoming a member of Congress he chaired the Southern Governors' Association, the Democratic Governors' Association, the Education Commission of the States, the Democratic Leadership Council, Jobs for America's Graduates, the National Conference of Lieutenant Governors, and the Virginia Forum on Education, and was President of the Council of State Governments.

During the 1960s he served on active duty with the United States Marine Corps, retiring from the Marine Corps Reserve in 1991. He began as the Class Honor Graduate from Marine Officers Basic School in 1961 and ended up as head of the principal recruiting program for Marine officers in 1970. In between, he served in both the 1st and 2nd Marine Divisions and his assignments included duty as a Military Social Aide at the White House and command of an infantry company in combat in Vietnam.

He received his law degree from the University of Virginia in 1973, clerked for Judge John D. Butzner, Jr., on the U.S. Court of Appeals for the Fourth Circuit, and practiced law with Williams and Connolly prior to his election to state office. Between his state and federal service he was a partner at Hunton and Williams.

Since leaving the Senate in 2001 he has served as Chairman of the Board of Visitors at the United States Naval Academy, Co-Chairman (with Senior Judge Laurence Silberman of the U.S. Court of Appeals for the D.C. Circuit) of the President's Commission on Intelligence Capabilities of the United States Regarding Weapons of Mass Destruction, and Co-Chairman (with former Governor Linwood Holton) of a major landowner's alliance that created a special tax district to finance the extension of Metrorail to Tyson's Corner, Reston, and Dulles Airport. He has also been a Fellow at the Institute of Politics at Harvard and at the Marshall Wythe School of Law at William and Mary.

He is currently on the President's Foreign Intelligence Advisory Board, the Secretary of State's International Security Advisory Board (Chairman of the WMD-Terrorism Task Force), the FBI Director's Advisory Board, the National Intelligence

Council's Strategic Analysis Advisory Board, the Iraq Study Group, and the MITRE Corp. Board of Trustees (Vice Chairman). He also serves on the boards of the Space Foundation, the Thomas Jefferson Program in Public Policy, the Concord Coalition, the National Museum of Americans at War, Strategic Partnerships LLC, and the Center for the Study of the Presidency—and he works on occasional projects with the Center for Strategic and International Studies. He is married to Lynda Johnson Robb and they have three grown daughters and one granddaughter.

Alan K. Simpson—Member

Alan K. Simpson served from 1979 to 1997 as a United States Senator from Wyoming. Following his first term in the Senate, Al was elected by his peers to the position of the Assistant Majority Leader in 1984—and served in that capacity until 1994. He completed his final term on January 3, 1997.

Simpson is currently a partner in the Cody firm of Simpson, Kepler and Edwards, the Cody division of the Denver firm of Burg Simpson Eldredge, Hersh and Jardine, and also a consultant in the Washington, D.C., government relations firm The Tongour, Simpson, Holsclaw Group. He continues to serve on numerous corporate and nonprofit boards and travels the country giving speeches. His book published by William Morrow Company, *Right in the Old Gazoo: A Lifetime of Scrapping with the Press* (1997), chronicles his personal experiences and views of the Fourth Estate.

From January of 1997 until June of 2000, Simpson was a Visiting Lecturer and for two years the Director of the Institute of Politics at Harvard University's John F. Kennedy School of Government. During the fall of 2000 he returned to his alma mater, the University of Wyoming, as a Visiting Lecturer in the

Political Science Department and he continues to team teach a class part-time with his brother, Peter, titled "Wyoming's Political Identity: Its History and Its Politics," which is proving to be one of the most popular classes offered at UW.

A member of a political family—his father served both as Governor of Wyoming from 1954 to 1958 and as United States Senator from Wyoming from 1962 to 1966—Al chose to follow in his father's footsteps and began his own political career in 1964 when he was elected to the Wyoming State Legislature as a state representative of his native Park County. He served for the next thirteen years in the Wyoming House of Representatives, holding the offices of Majority Whip, Majority Floor Leader, and Speaker Pro-Tem. His only brother, Peter, also served as a member of the Wyoming State Legislature.

Prior to entering politics, Simpson was admitted to the Wyoming bar and the United States District Court in 1958 and served for a short time as a Wyoming assistant attorney general. Simpson then joined his father, Milward L. Simpson, and later Charles G. Kepler in the law firm of Simpson, Kepler and Simpson in his hometown of Cody. He would practice law there for the next eighteen years. During that time, Simpson was very active in all civic, community, and state activities. He also served ten years as City Attorney.

Simpson earned a B.S. in law from the University of Wyoming in 1954. Upon graduation from college, he joined the Army, serving overseas in the 5th Infantry Division and in the 2nd Armored Division in the final months of the Army of Occupation in Germany. Following his honorable discharge in 1956, Simpson returned to the University of Wyoming to complete his study of law, earning his J.D. degree in 1958. He and his wife Ann have three children and six grandchildren, who all reside in Cody, Wyoming.

Iraq Study Group Support

Edward P. Djerejian
Senior Advisor to the Study Group

Christopher A. Kojm
Senior Advisor to the Study Group

John B. Williams   Benjamin J. Rhodes
Special Assistant to the Study Group   *Special Assistant to the Study Group*

United States Institute of Peace Support

Daniel P. Serwer
ISG Executive Director and Political Development Secretariat

Paul Hughes
Military and Security Secretariat

Gary Matthews
Economy and Reconstruction Secretariat

Paul Stares
Strategic Environment Secretariat

Courtney Rusin
Assistant to the Study Group

Anne Hingeley
Congressional Relations

Ian Larsen
Outreach and Communications

Center for the Study of the Presidency Support

Jay M. Parker
Advisor

Ysbrant A. Marcelis
Advisor

Center for Strategic & International Studies Support

Kay King
Advisor